5-31-23

The Aims of Education
and Other Essays

Alfred North Whitehead

D0059123

THE FREE PRESS
A Division of Macmillan, Inc.
NEW YORK

Maxwell Macmillan Canada
TORONTO

Maxwell Macmillan International
NEW YORK   OXFORD   SINGAPORE   SYDNEY

The Free Press
A Division of Macmillan, Inc.
866 Third Avenue, New York, N.Y. 10022

Maxwell Macmillan Canada, Inc.
1200 Eglinton Avenue East
Suite 200
Don Mills, Ontario M3C 3N1

Macmillan, Inc. is part of the Maxwell Communication
Group of Companies.

Library of Congress Catalog Card Number: 29-10164

First Free Press Paperback Edition 1967

Printed in the United States of America

printing number

22 23 24 25 26 27 28 29 30

Preface

The general topic of this volume is education on its intellectual side. One main idea runs through the various chapters, and is illustrated in them from many points of view. It can be stated briefly thus: The students are alive, and the purpose of education is to stimulate and guide their self-development. It follows as a corollary from this premiss, that the teachers also should be alive with living thoughts. The whole book is a protest against dead knowledge, that is to say, against inert ideas. The separate chapters have, with the exception of Chapter IX, been delivered as addresses at various conferences of educational bodies and of scientific societies. They are the outcome of practical experience, reflections on the practice of education and some criticisms on the meaning of the topics constituting its content.

The references to the educational system concern England. The failures and successes of the system in that country are somewhat different from those in America. But such references are merely illustrative: the general principles apply equally to both countries.

The earliest of the addresses was delivered in the year 1912 to the Educational Section of the International Congress of Mathematicians, meeting at Cambridge, England, and the latest in the year 1928 at the Business School of Harvard University, Cambridge, Massachusetts. Chapters I, IV, VI, VIII, IX, and X have been published in my book, *The Organisation of Thoughts* (Williams and Norgate, London, 1917). Chapter II, *The Rhythm of Education,* has been published as a separate pamphlet (Christophers, London, 1922). In this republication there are omissions but no other alterations. In particular, the three final chapters of the present book, with some omissions, stand as published in 1917. They are not to be constructed as commentaries on my writings since that date. The converse relation is the true one.

My thanks are due to the Editor of *The Hibbert Journal* for permission to republish Chapter III, *The Rhythmic Claims of Freedom and Discipline*, and Chapter V, *The Place of Classics in Education*, also to the Editor of *The Atlantic Monthly* for permission to republish Chapter VII, *Universities and Their Function*.

A. N. W.

Harvard University,
January, 1929.

Contents

The Aims of Education

CHAPTER I

The Aims of Education

Culture is activity of thought, and receptiveness to beauty and humane feeling. Scraps of information have nothing to do with it. A merely well-informed man is the most useless bore on God's earth. What we should aim at producing is men who possess both culture and expert knowledge in some special direction. Their expert knowledge will give them the ground to start from, and their culture will lead them as deep as philosophy and as high as art. We have to remember that the valuable intellectual development is self-development, and that it mostly takes place between the ages of sixteen and thirty. As to training, the most important part is given by mothers before the age of twelve. A saying due to Archbishop Temple illustrates my meaning. Surprise was expressed at the success in after-life of a man, who as a boy at Rugby had been somewhat undistinguished. He answered, "It is not what they are at eighteen, it is what they become afterwards that matters."

In training a child to activity of thought, above all things we must beware of what I will call "inert ideas"—that is to say, ideas that are merely received into the mind without being utilised, or tested, or thrown into fresh combinations.

In the history of education, the most striking phenomenon is that schools of learning, which at one epoch are alive with a ferment of genius, in a succeeding generation exhibit merely pedantry and routine. The reason is, that they are overladen with inert ideas. Education with inert ideas is not only useless: it is, above all things, harmful—*Corruptio optimi, pessima.* Except at rare intervals of intellectual ferment, education in the past has been radically infected with inert ideas. That is the reason why uneducated clever women, who have seen much of the world, are in middle life so much the most cultured part of the community. They have been saved from this horrible burden of inert ideas. Every intellectual revolution which has ever stirred humanity into greatness has been a passionate protest against inert ideas. Then, alas, with pathetic ignorance of human psychology, it has proceeded by some educational scheme to bind humanity afresh with inert ideas of its own fashioning.

Let us now ask how in our system of education we are to guard against this mental dryrot. We enunciate two educational commandments, "Do not teach too many subjects," and again, "What you teach, teach thoroughly."

The result of teaching small parts of a large number of subjects is the passive reception of disconnected ideas, not illumined with any spark of vitality. Let the main ideas which are introduced into a child's education be few and important, and let them be thrown into every combination possible. The child should make them his own, and should understand their application here and now in the circumstances of his actual life. From the very beginning of his education, the child should experience the joy of discovery. The discovery which he has to make, is that general ideas give an understanding of that stream of events which pours through his life, which is his life. By understanding I mean more than a mere logical analysis, though that is included. I mean "understanding" in the sense in which it is used in the French proverb, "To understand all, is to forgive all." Pedants sneer at an education which is useful. But if education is not useful, what is it? Is it a talent, to be hidden away in a napkin? Of course, education should be useful, whatever your aim in life. It was useful to Saint Augustine and it was useful to Napoleon. It is useful, because understanding is useful.

I pass lightly over that understanding which should be given by the literary side of education. Nor do I wish to be supposed to pronounce on the relative merits of a classical or a modern curriculum. I would only remark that the understanding which we want is an understanding of an insistent present. The only use of a knowledge of the past is to equip us for the present. No more deadly harm can be done to young minds than by depreciation of the present. The present contains all that there is. It is holy ground; for it is the past, and it is the future. At the same time it must be observed that an age is no less past if it existed two hundred years ago than if it existed two thousand years ago. Do not be deceived by the pedantry of dates. The ages of Shakespeare and of Molière are no less past than are the ages of Sophocles and of Virgil. The communion of saints is a great and inspiring assemblage, but it has only one possible hall of meeting, and that is, the present; and the mere lapse of time through which any particular group of saints must travel to reach that meeting-place, makes very little difference.

Passing now to the scientific and logical side of education, we remember that here also ideas which are not utilised are positively harmful. By utilising an idea, I mean relating it to that stream, compounded of sense perceptions, feelings, hopes, desires, and of mental activities adjusting thought to thought, which forms our life. I can imagine a set of beings which might fortify their souls by passively reviewing disconnected ideas. Humanity is not built that way—except perhaps some editors of newspapers.

In scientific training, the first thing to do with an idea is to prove it. But allow me for one moment to extend the meaning of "prove"; I mean—to prove its worth. Now an idea is not worth much unless the propositions in which it is embodied are true. Accordingly an essential part of the proof of an idea is the proof, either by experiment or by logic, of the truth of the propositions. But it is not essential that this proof of the truth should constitute the first introduction to the idea. After all, its assertion by the authority of respectable teachers is sufficient evidence to begin with. In our first contact with a set of propositions, we commence by appreciating their importance. That is what we all do in after-life. We do not attempt, in the strict sense, to prove or to disprove anything, unless its importance makes it worthy of that honour. These two processes of proof, in the narrow sense, and of appreciation, do not require a rigid separation in time. Both can be proceeded with nearly concurrently. But in so far as either process must have the priority, it should be that of appreciation by use.

Furthermore, we should not endeavour to use propositions in isolation. Emphatically I do not mean, a neat little set of experiments to illustrate Proposition I and then the proof of Proposition I, a neat little set of experiments to illustrate Proposition II and then the proof of Proposition II, and so on to the end of the book. Nothing could be more boring. Interrelated truths are utilised *en bloc,* and the various propositions are employed in any order, and with any reiteration. Choose some important applications of your theoretical subject; and study them concurrently with the systematic theoretical exposition. Keep the theoretical exposition short and simple, but let it be strict and rigid so far as it goes. It should not be too long for it to be easily known with thoroughness and accuracy. The consequences of a plethora of half-digested theoretical knowledge are deplorable. Also the theory should not be muddled up with the practice. The child should have no doubt when it is proving and when it is utilising. My point is that what is proved should be utilised, and that what is utilised should—so far as is practicable—be proved. I am far from asserting that proof and utilisation are the same thing.

At this point of my discourse, I can most directly carry forward my argument in the outward form of a digression. We are only just realising that the art and science of education require a genius and a study of their own; and that this genius and this science are more than a bare knowledge of some branch of science or of literature. This truth was partially perceived in the past generation; and headmasters, somewhat crudely, were apt to supersede learning in their colleagues by requiring left-hand bowling and a taste for football. But culture is more than cricket, and more than football, and more than extent of knowledge.

Education is the acquisition of the art of the utilisation of knowledge. This is an art very difficult to impart. Whenever a textbook is written of real educational worth, you may be quite certain that some reviewer will say that it will be difficult to teach from it. Of course it will be difficult to teach from it. If it were easy, the book ought to be burned; for it cannot be educational. In education, as elsewhere, the broad primrose path leads to a nasty place. This evil path is represented by a book or a set of lectures which will practically enable the student to learn by heart all the questions likely to be asked at the next external examination. And I may say in passing that no educational system is possible unless every question directly asked of a pupil at any examination is either framed or modified by the actual teacher of that pupil in that subject. The external assessor may report on the curriculum or on the performance of the pupils, but never should be allowed to ask the pupil a question which has not been strictly supervised by the actual teacher, or at least inspired by a long conference with him. There are a few exceptions to this rule, but they are exceptions, and could easily be allowed for under the general rule.

We now return to my previous point, that theoretical ideas should always find important applications within the pupil's curriculum. This is not an easy doctrine to apply, but a very hard one. It contains within itself the problem of keeping knowledge alive, of preventing it from becoming inert, which is the central problem of all education.

The best procedure will depend on several factors, none of which can be neglected, namely, the genius of the teacher, the intellectual type of the pupils, their prospects in life, the opportunities offered by the immediate surroundings of the school, and allied factors of this sort. It is for this reason that the uniform external examination is so deadly. We do not denounce it because we are cranks, and like denouncing established things. We are not so childish. Also, of course, such examinations have their use in testing slackness. Our reason of dislike is very definite and very practical. It kills the best part of culture. When you analyse in the light of experience the central task of education, you find that its successful accomplishment depends on a delicate adjustment of many variable factors. The reason is that we are dealing with human minds, and not with dead matter. The evocation of curiosity, of judgment, of the power of mastering a complicated tangle of circumstances, the use of theory in giving foresight in special cases—all these powers are not to be imparted by a set rule embodied in one schedule of examination subjects.

I appeal to you, as practical teachers. With good discipline, it is always possible to pump into the minds of a class a certain quantity of inert knowledge. You take a text-book and make them learn it. So far, so good. The child then knows how to solve a quadratic equation. But what is the point of teaching a child to solve a quadratic equation? There is a traditional answer to this question. It runs thus: The mind is an instrument, you first sharpen it, and then use it; the acquisition of the power of solving a quadratic equation is part of the process of sharpening the mind. Now there is just enough truth in this answer to have made it live through the ages. But for all its half-truth, it embodies a radical error which bids fair to stifle the genius of the modern world. I do not know who was first responsible for this analogy of the mind to a dead instrument. For aught I know, it may have been one of the seven wise men of Greece, or a committee of the whole lot of them. Whoever was the originator, there can be no doubt of the authority which it has acquired by the continuous approval bestowed upon it by eminent persons. But whatever its weight of authority, whatever the high approval which it can quote, I have no hesitation in denouncing it as one of the most fatal, erroneous, and dangerous conceptions ever introduced into the theory of education. The mind is never passive; it is a perpetual activity, delicate, receptive, responsive to stimulus. You cannot postpone its life until you have sharpened it. Whatever interest attaches to your subject-matter must be evoked here and now; whatever powers you are strengthening in the pupil, must be exercised here and now; whatever possibilities of mental life your teaching should impart, must be exhibited here and now. That is the golden rule of education, and a very difficult rule to follow.

The difficulty is just this: the apprehension of general ideas, intellectual habits of mind, and pleasurable interest in mental achievement can be evoked by no form of words, however accurately adjusted. All practical teachers know that education is a patient process of the mastery of details, minute by minute, hour by hour, day by day. There is no royal road to learning through an airy path of brilliant generalisations. There is a proverb about the difficulty of seeing the wood because of the trees. That difficulty is exactly the point which I am enforcing. The problem of education is to make the pupil see the wood by means of the trees.

The solution which I am urging, is to eradicate the fatal disconnection of subjects which kills the vitality of our modern curriculum. There is only one subject-matter for education, and that is

Life in all its manifestations. Instead of this single unity, we offer children—Algebra, from which nothing follows; Geometry, from which nothing follows; Science, from which nothing follows; History, from which nothing follows; a Couple of Languages, never mastered; and lastly, most dreary of all, Literature, represented by plays of Shakespeare, with philological notes and short analyses of plot and character to be in substance committed to memory. Can such a list be said to represent Life, as it is known in the midst of the living of it? The best that can be said of it is, that it is a rapid table of contents which a deity might run over in his mind while he was thinking of creating a world, and has not yet determined how to put it together.

Let us now return to quadratic equations. We still have on hand the unanswered question. Why should children be taught their solution? Unless quadratic equations fit into a connected curriculum, of course there is no reason to teach anything about them. Furthermore, extensive as should be the place of mathematics in a complete culture, I am a little doubtful whether for many types of boys algebraic solutions of quadratic equations do not lie on the specialist side of mathematics. I may here remind you that as yet I have not said anything of the psychology or the content of the specialism, which is so necessary a part of an ideal education. But all that is an evasion of our real question, and I merely state it in order to avoid being misunderstood in my answer.

Quadratic equations are part of algebra, and algebra is the intellectual instrument which has been created for rendering clear the quantitative aspects of the world. There is no getting out of it. Through and through the world is infected with quantity. To talk sense, is to talk in quantities. It is no use saying that the nation is large,—How large? It is no use saying that radium is scarce,—How scarce? You cannot evade quantity. You may fly to poetry and to music, and quantity and number will face you in your rhythms and your octaves. Elegant intellects which despise the theory of quantity, are but half developed. They are more to be pitied than blamed. The scraps of gibberish, which in their school-days were taught to them in the name of algebra, deserve some contempt.

This question of the degeneration of algebra into gibberish, both in word and in fact, affords a pathetic instance of the uselessness of reforming educational schedules without a clear conception of the attributes which you wish to evoke in the living minds of the children. A few years ago there was an outcry that school algebra was in need of reform, but there was a general agreement that graphs would put everything right. So all sorts of things were extruded, and graphs were introduced. So far as I can see, with no sort of idea behind them, but just graphs. Now every examination paper has one or two questions on graphs. Personally I am an enthusiastic adherent of graphs. But I wonder whether as yet we have gained very much. You cannot put life into any schedule of general education unless you succeed in exhibiting its relation to some essential characteristic of all intelligent or emotional perception. It is a hard saying, but it is true; and I do not see how to make it any easier. In making these little formal alterations you are beaten by the very nature of things. You are pitted against too skilful an adversary, who will see to it that the pea is always under the other thimble.

Reformation must begin at the other end. First, you must make up your mind as to those quantitative aspects of the world which are simple enough to be introduced into general education; then a schedule of algebra should be framed which will about find its exemplification in these applications. We need not fear for our pet graphs, they will be there in plenty when we once begin to treat algebra as a serious means of studying the world. Some of the simplest applications will be found in the quantities which occur in the simplest study of society. The curves of history are more vivid and more informing than the dry catalogues of names and dates which comprise the greater part of that arid school study. What purpose is effected by a catalogue of undistinguished kings and queens? Tom, Dick, or Harry, they are all dead. General resurrections are failures, and are better postponed. The quantitative flux of the forces of modern society is capable of very simple exhibition. Meanwhile, the idea of the variable, of the function, of rate of change, of equations and their solution, of elimination, are being studied as an abstract science for their own sake. Not, of course, in the pompous phrases with which I am alluding to them here, but with that iteration of simple special cases proper to teaching.

If this course be followed, the route from Chaucer to the Black

Death, from the Black Death to modern Labour troubles, will connect the tales of the mediæval pilgrims with the abstract science of algebra, both yielding diverse aspects of that single theme, Life. I know what most of you are thinking at this point. It is that the exact course which I have sketched out is not the particular one which you would have chosen, or even see how to work. I quite agree. I am not claiming that I could do it myself. But your objection is the precise reason why a common external examination system is fatal to education. The process of exhibiting the applications of knowledge must, for its success, essentially depend on the character of the pupils and the genius of the teacher. Of course I have left out the easiest applications with which most of us are more at home. I mean the quantitative sides of sciences, such as mechanics and physics.

Again, in the same connection we plot the statistics of social phenomena against the time. We then eliminate the time between suitable pairs. We can speculate how far we have exhibited a real causal connection, or how far a mere temporal coincidence. We notice that we might have plotted against the time one set of statistics for one country and another set for another country, and thus, with suitable choice of subjects, have obtained graphs which certainly exhibited mere coincidence. Also other graphs exhibit obvious causal connections. We wonder how to discriminate. And so are drawn on as far as we will.

But in considering this description, I must beg you to remember what I have been insisting on above. In the first place, one train of thought will not suit all groups of children. For example, I should expect that artisan children will want something more concrete and, in a sense, swifter than I have set down here. Perhaps I am wrong, but that is what I should guess. In the second place, I am not contemplating one beautiful lecture stimulating, once and for all, an admiring class. That is not the way in which education proceeds. No; all the time the pupils are hard at work solving examples, drawing graphs, and making experiments, until they have a thorough hold on the whole subject. I am describing the interspersed explanations, the directions which should be given to their thoughts. The pupils have got to be made to feel that they are studying something, and are not merely executing intellectual minuets.

Finally, if you are teaching pupils for some general examination, the problem of sound teaching is greatly complicated. Have you ever noticed the zig-zag moulding round a Norman arch? The ancient work is beautiful, the modern work is hideous. The reason is, that the modern work is done to exact measure, the ancient work is varied according to the idiosyncrasy of the workman. Here it is crowded, and there it is expanded. Now the essence of getting pupils through examinations is to give equal weight to all parts of the schedule. But mankind is naturally specialist. One man sees a whole subject, where another can find only a few detached examples. I know that it seems contradictory to allow for specialism in a curriculum especially designed for a broad culture. Without contradictions the world would be simpler, and perhaps duller. But I am certain that in education wherever you exclude specialism you destroy life.

We now come to the other great branch of a general mathematical education, namely Geometry. The same principles apply. The theoretical part should be clear-cut, rigid, short, and important. Every proposition not absolutely necessary to exhibit the main connection of ideas should be cut out, but the great fundamental ideas should be all there. No omission of concepts, such as those of Similarity and Proportion. We must remember that, owing to the aid rendered by the visual presence of a figure, Geometry is a field of unequalled excellence for the exercise of the deductive faculties of reasoning. Then, of course, there follows Geometrical Drawing, with its training for the hand and eye.

But, like Algebra, Geometry and Geometrical Drawing must be extended beyond the mere circle of geometrical ideas. In an industrial neighbourhood, machinery and workshop practice form the appropriate extension. For example, in the London Polytechnics this has been achieved with conspicuous success. For many secondary schools I suggest that surveying and maps are the natural applications. In particular, plane-table surveying should lead pupils to a vivid apprehension of the immediate application of geometric truths. Simple drawing apparatus, a surveyor's chain, and a surveyor's compass, should enable the pupils to rise from the survey and mensuration of a field to the construction of the map of a small district. The best education is to be found in gaining the utmost information from the simplest apparatus. The provision of elaborate instruments is greatly to be deprecated. To have constructed the map of a small district, to have considered its roads, its contours, its geology, its climate, its relation to other districts, the effects on the status of its inhabitants, will teach more history and geography than any knowledge of Perkin Warbeck or of Behren's Straits. I mean not a nebulous lecture on the subject, but a serious investigation in which the real facts are definitely ascertained by the aid of accurate theoretical knowledge. A typical mathematical problem should be: Survey such and such a field, draw a plan of it to such and such a scale, and find the area. It would be quite a good procedure to impart the necessary geometrical propositions without their proofs. Then, concurrently in the same term, the proofs of the propositions would be learnt while the survey was being made.

Fortunately, the specialist side of education presents an easier problem than does the provision of a general culture. For this there are many reasons. One is that many of the principles of procedure to be observed are the same in both cases, and it is unnecessary to recapitulate. Another reason is that specialist training takes place— or should take place—at a more advanced stage of the pupil's course, and thus there is easier material to work upon. But undoubtedly the chief reason is that the specialist study is normally a study of peculiar interest to the student. He is studying it because, for some reason, he wants to know it. This makes all the difference. The general culture is designed to foster an activity of mind; the specialist course utilises this activity. But it does not do to lay too much stress on these neat antitheses. As we have already seen, in the general course foci of special interest will arise; and similarly in the special study, the external connections of the subject drag thought outwards.

Again, there is not one course of study which merely gives general culture, and another which gives special knowledge. The subjects pursued for the sake of a general education are special subjects specially studied; and, on the other hand, one of the ways of encouraging general mental activity is to foster a special devotion. You may not divide the seamless coat of learning. What education has to impart is an intimate sense for the power of ideas, for the beauty of ideas, and for the structure of ideas, together with a particular body of knowledge which has peculiar reference to the life of the being possessing it.

The appreciation of the structure of ideas is that side of a cultured mind which can only grow under the influence of a special study. I mean that eye for the whole chess-board, for the bearing of one set of ideas on another. Nothing but a special study can give any appreciation for the exact formulation of general ideas, for their relations when formulated, for their service in the comprehension of life. A mind so disciplined should be both more abstract and more concrete. It has been trained in the comprehension of abstract thought and in the analysis of facts.

Finally, there should grow the most austere of all mental qualities; I mean the sense for style. It is an æsthetic sense, based on admiration for the direct attainment of a foreseen end, simply and without waste. Style in art, style in literature, style in science, style in logic, style in practical execution have fundamentally the same aesthetic qualities, namely, attainment and restraint. The love of a subject in itself and for itself, where it is not the sleepy pleasure of pacing a mental quarter-deck, is the love of style as manifested in that study.

Here we are brought back to the position from which we started, the utility of education. Style, in its finest sense, is the last acquirement of the educated mind; it is also the most useful. It pervades the whole being. The administrator with a sense for style hates waste; the engineer with a sense for style economises his material; the artisan with a sense for style prefers good work. Style is the ultimate morality of mind.

But above style, and above knowledge, there is something, a vague shape like fate above the Greek gods. That something is Power. Style is the fashioning of power, the restraining of power. But, after all, the power of attainment of the desired end is fundamental. The first thing is to get there. Do not bother about your style, but solve your problem, justify the ways of God to man, administer your province, or do whatever else is set before you.

Where, then, does style help? In this, with style the end is attained without side issues, without raising undesirable inflammations. With style you attain your end and nothing but your end.

With style the effect of your activity is calculable, and foresight is the last gift of gods to men. With style your power is increased, for your mind is not distracted with irrelevancies, and you are more likely to attain your object. Now style is the exclusive privilege of the expert. Whoever heard of the style of an amateur painter, of the style of an amateur poet? Style is always the product of specialist study, the peculiar contribution of specialism to culture.

English education in its present phase suffers from a lack of definite aim, and from an external machinery which kills its vitality. Hitherto in this address I have been considering the aims which should govern education. In this respect England halts between two opinions. It has not decided whether to produce amateurs or experts. The profound change in the world which the nineteenth century has produced is that the growth of knowledge has given foresight. The amateur is essentially a man with appreciation and with immense versatility in mastering a given routine. But he lacks the foresight which comes from special knowledge. The object of this address is to suggest how to produce the expert without loss of the essential virtues of the amateur. The machinery of our secondary education is rigid where it should be yielding, and lax where it should be rigid. Every school is bound on pain of extinction to train its boys for a small set of definite examinations. No headmaster has a free hand to develop his general education or his specialist studies in accordance with the opportunities of his school, which are created by its staff, its environment, its class of boys, and its endowments. I suggest that no system of external tests which aims primarily at examining individual scholars can result in anything but educational waste.

Primarily it is the schools and not the scholars which should be inspected. Each school should grant its own leaving certificates, based on its own curriculum. The standards of these schools should be sampled and corrected. But the first requisite for educational reform is the school as a unit, with its approved curriculum based on its own needs, and evolved by its own staff. If we fail to secure that, we simply fall from one formalism into another, from one dung-hill of inert ideas into another.

In stating that the school is the true educational unit in any national system for the safeguarding of efficiency, I have conceived the alternative system as being the external examination of the individual scholar. But every Scylla is faced by its Charybdis—or, in more homely language, there is a ditch on both sides of the road. It will be equally fatal to education if we fall into the hands of a supervising department which is under the impression that it can divide all schools into two or three rigid categories, each type being forced to adopt a rigid curriculum. When I say that the school is the educational unit, I mean exactly what I say, no larger unit, no smaller unit. Each school must have the claim to be considered in relation to its special circumstances. The classifying of schools for some purposes is necessary. But no absolutely rigid curriculum, not modified by its own staff, should be permissible. Exactly the same principles apply, with the proper modifications, to universities and to technical colleges.

When one considers in its length and in its breadth the importance of this question of the education of a nation's young, the broken lives, the defeated hopes, the national failures, which result from the frivolous inertia with which it is treated, it is difficult to restrain within oneself a savage rage. In the conditions of modern life the rule is absolute, the race which does not value trained intelligence is doomed. Not all your heroism, not all your social charm, not all your wit, not all your victories on land or at sea, can move back the finger of fate. To-day we maintain ourselves. To-morrow science will have moved forward yet one more step, and there will be no appeal from the judgment which will then be pronounced on the uneducated.

We can be content with no less than the old summary of educational ideal which has been current at any time from the dawn of our civilisation. The essence of education is that it be religious.

Pray, what is religious education?

A religious education is an education which inculcates duty and reverence. Duty arises from our potential control over the course of events. Where attainable knowledge could have changed the issue, ignorance has the guilt of vice. And the foundation of reverence is this perception, that the present holds within itself the complete sum of existence, backwards and forwards, that whole amplitude of time, which is eternity.

CHAPTER II

The Rhythm of Education

By the Rhythm of Education I denote a certain principle which in its practical application is well known to everyone with educational experience. Accordingly, when I remember that I am speaking to an audience of some of the leading educationalists in England, I have no expectation that I shall be saying anything that is new to you. I do think, however, that the principle has not been subjected to an adequate discussion taking account of all the factors which should guide its application.

I first seek for the baldest statement of what I mean by the Rhythm of Education, a statement so bald as to exhibit the point of this address in its utter obviousness. The principle is merely this—that different subjects and modes of study should be undertaken by pupils at fitting times when they have reached the proper stage of mental development. You will agree with me that this is a truism, never doubted and known to all. I am really anxious to emphasise the obvious character of the foundational idea of my address; for one reason, because this audience will certainly find it out for itself. But the other reason, the reason why I choose this subject for discourse, is that I do not think that this obvious truth has been handled in educational practice with due attention to the psychology of the pupils.

The Tasks of Infancy

I commence by challenging the adequacy of some principles by which the subjects for study are often classified in order. By this I

15

mean that these principles can only be accepted as correct if they are so explained as to be explained away. Consider first the criterion of difficulty. It is not true that the easier subjects should precede the harder. On the contrary, some of the hardest must come first because nature so dictates, and because they are essential to life. The first intellectual task which confronts an infant is the acquirement of spoken language. What an appalling task, the correlation of meanings with sounds! It requires an anlysis of ideas and an analysis of sounds. We all know that the infant does it, and that the miracle of his achievement is explicable. But so are all miracles, and yet to the wise they remain miracles. All I ask is that with this example staring us in the face we should cease talking nonsense about postponing the harder subjects.

What is the next subject in the education of the infant minds? The acquirement of written language; that is to say, the correlation of sounds with shapes. Great heavens! Have our educationists gone mad? They are setting babbling mites of six years old to tasks which might daunt a sage after lifelong toil. Again, the hardest task in mathematics is the study of the elements of algebra, and yet this stage must precede the comparative simplicity of the differential calculus.

I will not elaborate my point further; I merely restate it in the form, that the postponement of difficulty is no safe clue for the maze of educational practice.

The alternative principle of order among subjects is that of necessary antecedence. There we are obviously on firmer ground. It is impossible to read *Hamlet* until you can read; and the study of integers must precede the study of fractions. And yet even this firm principle dissolves under scrutiny. It is certainly true, but it is only true if you give an artificial limitation to the concept of a subject for study. The danger of the principle is that it is accepted in one sense, for which it is almost a necessary truth, and that it is applied in another sense for which it is false. You cannot read Homer before you can read; but many a child, and in ages past many a man, has sailed with Odysseus over the seas of Romance by the help of the spoken word of a mother, or of some wandering bard. The uncritical application of the principle of the necessary antecedence of some subjects to others has, in the hands of dull people with a turn for organisation, produced in education the dryness of the Sahara.

Stages of Mental Growth

The reason for the title which I have chosen for this address, the Rhythm of Education, is derived from yet another criticism of current ideas. The pupil's progress is often conceived as a uniform steady advance undifferentiated by change of type or alteration in pace; for example, a boy may be conceived as starting Latin at ten years of age and by a uniform progression steadily developing into a classical scholar at the age of eighteen or twenty. I hold that this conception of education is based upon a false psychology of the process of mental development which has gravely hindered the effectiveness of our methods. Life is essentially periodic. It comprises daily periods, with their alternations of work and play, of activity and of sleep, and seasonal periods, which dictate our terms and our holidays; and also it is composed of well-marked yearly periods. These are the gross obvious periods which no one can overlook. There are also subtler periods of mental growth, with their cyclic recurrences, yet always different as we pass from cycle to cycle, though the subordinate stages are reproduced in each cycle. That is why I have chosen the term "rhythmic," as meaning essentially the conveyance of difference within a framework of repetition. Lack of attention to the rhythm and character of mental growth is a main source of wooden futility in education. I think that Hegel was right when he analysed progress into three stages, which he called Thesis, Antithesis, and Synthesis; though for the purpose of the application of his idea to educational theory I do not think that the names he gave are very happily suggestive. In relation to intellectual progress I would term them, the stage of romance, the stage of precision, and the stage of generalisation.

The Stage of Romance

The stage of romance is the stage of first apprehension. The subject-matter has the vividness of novelty; it holds within itself unexplored connexions with possibilities half-disclosed by glimpses and half-concealed by the wealth of material. In this stage knowledge is not dominated by systematic procedure. Such system as there must be is created piecemeal *ad hoc*. We are in the presence of immediate cognisance of fact, only intermittently subjecting fact to systematic dissection. Romantic emotion is essentially the excitement consequent on the transition from the bare facts to the first realisations of the import of their unexplored relationships. For example, Crusoe was a mere man, the sand was mere sand, the footprint was a mere footprint, and the island a mere island, and Europe was the busy world of men. But the sudden perception of the half-disclosed and half-hidden possibilities relating Crusoe and the sand and the footprint and the lonely island secluded from Europe constitutes romance. I have had to take an extreme case for illustration in order to make my meaning perfectly plain. But construe it as an allegory representing the first stage in a cycle of progress. Education must essentially be a setting in order of a ferment already stirring in the mind: you cannot educate mind in *vacuo*. In our conception of education we tend to confine it to the second stage of the cycle; namely, to the stage of precision. But we cannot so limit our task without misconceiving the whole problem. We are concerned alike with the ferment, with the acquirement of precision, and with the subsequent fruition.

The Stage of Precision

The stage of precision also represents an addition to knowledge. In this stage, width of relationship is subordinated to exactness of formulation. It is the stage of grammar, the grammar of language and the grammar of science. It proceeds by forcing on the students' acceptance a given way of analysing the facts, bit by bit. New facts are added, but they are the facts which fit into the analysis.

It is evident that a stage of precision is barren without a previous stage of romance: unless there are facts which have already been vaguely apprehended in their broad generality, the previous analysis is an analysis of nothing. It is simply a series of meaningless statements about bare facts, produced artificially and without any further relevance. I repeat that in this stage we do not merely remain within the circle of the facts elicited in the romantic epoch. The facts of romance have disclosed ideas with possibilities of wide significance, and in the stage of precise progress we acquire other facts in a systematic order, which thereby form both a disclosure and an analysis of the general subject-matter of the romance.

The Stage of Generalisation

The final stage of generalisation is Hegel's synthesis. It is a return to romanticism with added advantage of classified ideas and relevant technique. It is the fruition which has been the goal of the precise training. It is the final success. I am afraid that I have had to give a dry analysis of somewhat obvious ideas. It has been necessary to do so because my subsequent remarks presuppose that we have clearly in our minds the essential character of this threefold cycle.

The Cyclic Processes

Education should consist in a continual repetition of such cycles. Each lesson in its minor way should form an eddy cycle issuing in its own subordinate process. Longer periods should issue in definite attainments, which then form the starting-grounds for fresh cycles. We should banish the idea of a mythical, far-off end of education. The pupils must be continually enjoying some fruition and starting afresh—if the teacher is stimulating in exact proportion to his success in satisfying the rhythmic cravings of his pupils.

An infant's first romance is its awakening to the apprehension of objects and to the appreciation of their connexions. Its growth in mentality takes the exterior form of occupying itself in the co-ordination of its perceptions with its bodily activities. Its first stage of precision is mastering spoken language as an instrument for classifying its contemplation of objects and for strengthening its apprehension of emotional relations with other beings. Its first stage of generalisation is the use of language for a classified and enlarged enjoyment of objects.

This first cycle of intellectual progress from the achievement of perception to the acquirement of language, and from the acquirement of language to classified thought and keener perception, will bear more careful study. It is the only cycle of progress which we can observe in its purely natural state. The later cycles are necessarily tinged by the procedure of the current mode of education.

There is a characteristic of it which is often sadly lacking in subsequent education; I mean, that it achieves complete success. At the end of it the child *can* speak, its ideas *are* classified, and its perceptions *are* sharpened. The cycle achieves its object. This is a great deal more than can be said for most systems of education as applied to most pupils. But why should this be so? Certainly, a new-born baby looks a most unpromising subject for intellectual progress when we remember the difficulty of the task before it. I suppose it is because nature, in the form of surrounding circumstances, sets it a task for which the normal development of its brain is exactly fitted. I do not think that there is any particular mystery about the fact of a child learning to speak and in consequence thinking all the better; but it does offer food for reflection.

In the subsequent education we have not sought for cyclic processes which in a finite time run their course and within their own limited sphere achieve a complete success. This completion is one outstanding character in the natural cycle for infants. Later on we start a child on some subject, say Latin, at the age of ten, and hope by a uniform system of formal training to achieve success at the age of twenty. The natural result is failure, both in interest and in acquirement. When I speak of failure, I am comparing our results with the brilliant success of the first natural cycle. I do not think that. it is because our tasks are intrinsically too hard, when I remember that the infant's cycle is the hardest of all. It is because our tasks are set in an unnatural way, without rhythm and without the stimulus of intermediate successes and without concentration.

I have not yet spoken of this character of concentration which so conspicuously attaches to the infant's progress. The whole being of the infant is absorbed in the practice of its cycle. It has nothing else to divert its mental development. In this respect there is a striking difference between this natural cycle and the subsequent history of the student's development. It is perfectly obvious that life is very various and that the mind and brain naturally develop so as to adapt themselves to the many-hued world in which their lot is cast. Still, after making allowance for this consideration, we will be wise to preserve some measure of concentration for each of the subsequent cycles. In particular, we should avoid a competition of diverse subjects in the same stage of their cycles. The fault of the older education was unrhythmic concentration on a single undifferentiated subject. Our modern system, with its insistence on a preliminary general education, and with its easy toleration of the analysis of knowledge into distinct subjects, is an equally unrhythmic collection of distracting scraps. I am pleading that we shall endeavour to weave in the learner's mind a harmony of patterns, by co-ordinating the various elements of instruction into subordinate cycles each of intrinsic worth for the immediate apprehension of the pupil. We must garner our crops each in its due season.

The Romance of Adolescence

We will now pass to some concrete applications of the ideas which have been developed in the former part of my address.

The first cycle of infancy is succeeded by the cycle of adolescence, which opens with by far the greatest stage of romance which we ever experience. It is in this stage that the lines of character are graven. How the child emerges from the romantic stage of adolescence is how the subsequent life will be moulded by ideals and coloured by imagination. It rapidly follows on the generalisation of capacity produced by the acquirement of spoken language and of reading. The stage of generalisation belonging to the infantile cycle is comparatively short because the romantic material of infancy is so scanty. The initial knowledge of the world in any developed sense of the word "knowledge" really commences after the achievement of the first cycle, and thus issues in the tremendous age of romance. Ideas, facts, relationships, stories, histories, possibilities, artistry in words, in sounds, in form and in colour, crowd into the child's life, stir his feelings, excite his appreciation, and incite his impulses to kindred activities. It is a saddening thought that on this golden age there falls so often the shadow of the crammer. I am thinking of a period of about four years of the child's life, roughly, in ordinary cases, falling between the ages of eight and twelve or thirteen. It is the first great period of the utilisation of the native language, and of developed powers of observation and of manipulation. The infant cannot manipulate, the child can; the infant cannot observe, the child can; the infant cannot retain thoughts by the recollection of words, the child can. The child thus enters upon a new world.

Of course, the stage of precision prolongs itself as recurring in minor cycles which form eddies in the great romance. The perfecting of writing, of spelling, of the elements of arithmetic, and of lists of simple facts, such as the Kings of England, are all elements of precision, very necessary both as training in concentration and as useful acquirements. However, these are essentially fragmentary in character, whereas the great romance is the flood which bears on the child towards the life of the spirit.

The success of the Montessori system is due to its recognition of the dominance of romance at this period of growth. If this be the explanation, it also points to the limitations in the usefulness of that method. It is the system which in some measure is essential for every romantic stage. Its essence is browsing and the encouragement of vivid freshness. But it lacks the restraint which is necessary for the great stages of precision.

The Mastery of Language

As he nears the end of the great romance the cyclic course of growth is swinging the child over towards an aptitude for exact knowledge. Language is now the natural subject-matter for concentrated attack. It is the mode of expression with which he is thoroughly familiar. He is acquainted with stories, histories, and poems illustrating the lives of other people and of other civilisations. Accordingly, from the age of eleven onwards there is wanted a gradually increasing concentration towards precise knowledge of language. Finally, the three years from twelve to fifteen should be dominated by a mass attack upon language, so planned that a definite result, in itself worth having, is thereby achieved. I should guess that within these limits of time, and given adequate concentration, we might ask that at the end of that period the children should have command of English, should be able to read fluently fairly simple French, and should have completed the elementary stage of Latin; I mean, a precise knowledge of the more straightforward parts of Latin grammar, the knowledge of the construction of Latin sentences, and the reading of some parts of appropriate

Latin authors, perhaps simplified and largely supplemented by the aid of the best literary translations so that their reading of the original, plus translation, gives them a grip of the book as a literary whole. I conceive that such a measure of attainment in these three languages is well within the reach of the ordinary child, provided that he has not been distracted by the effort at precision in a multiplicity of other subjects. Also some more gifted children could go further. The Latin would come to them easily, so that it would be possible to start Greek before the end of the period, always provided that their bent is literary and that they mean later to pursue that study at least for some years. Other subjects will occupy a subordinate place in the time-table and will be undertaken in a different spirit. In the first place, it must be remembered that the semi-literary subjects, such as history, will largely have been provided in the study of the languages. It will be hardly possible to read some English, French, and Latin literature without imparting some knowledge of European history. I do not mean that all special history teaching should be abandoned. I do, however, suggest that the subject should be exhibited in what I have termed the romantic spirit, and that the pupils should not be subjected to the test of precise recollection of details on any large systematic scale.

At this period of growth science should be in its stage of romance. The pupils should see for themselves, and experiment for themselves, with only fragmentary precision of thought. The essence of the importance of science, both for interest in theory or for technological purposes, lies in its application to concrete detail, and every such application evokes a novel problem for research. Accordingly, all training in science should begin as well as end in research, and in getting hold of the subject-matter as it occurs in nature. The exact form of guidance suitable to this age and the exact limitations of experiment are matters depending on experience. But I plead that this period is the true age for the romance of science.

Concentration on Science

Towards the age of fifteen the age of precision in language and of romance in science draws to its close, to be succeeded by a period

of generalisation in language and of precision in science. This
should be a short period, but one of vital importance. I am thinking
of about one year's work, and I suggest that it would be well
decisively to alter the balance of the preceding curriculum. There
should be a concentration on science and a decided diminution of
the linguistic work. A year's work on science, coming on the top
of the previous romantic study, should make everyone understand
the main principles which govern the development of mechanics,
physics, chemistry, algebra and geometry. Understand that they are
not beginning these subjects, but they are putting together a
previous discursive study by an exact formulation of their main
ideas. For example, take algebra and geometry, which I single
out as being subjects with which I have some slight familiarity. In
the previous three years there has been work on the applications
of the simplest algebraic formulæ and geometrical propositions to
problems of surveying, or of some other scientific work involving
calculations. In this way arithmetic has been carefully strengthened
by the insistence on definite numerical results, and familiarity with
the ideas of literal formulæ and of geometrical properties has been
gained; also some minor methods of manipulation have been
inculcated. There is thus no long time to be wasted in getting used
to the ideas of the sciences. The pupils are ready for the small body
of algebraic and geometrical truths which they ought to know
thoroughly. Furthermore, in the previous period some boys will
have shown an aptitude for mathematics and will have pushed on
a little more, besides in the final year somewhat emphasising their
mathematics at the expense of some of the other subjects. I am
simply taking mathematics as an illustration.

Meanwhile, the cycle of language is in its stage of generalisation.
In this stage the precise study of grammar and composition is dis-
continued, and the language study is confined to reading the literature with emphasised attention to its ideas and to the general history
in which it is embedded; also the time allotted to history will pass
into the precise study of a short definite period, chosen to illustrate
exactly what does happen at an important epoch and also to show
how to pass the simpler types of judgments on men and policies.

I have now sketched in outline the course of education from baby-
hood to about sixteen and a half, arranged with some attention to

the rhythmic pulses of life. In some such way a general education is possible in which the pupil throughout has the advantage of concentration and of freshness. Thus precision will always illustrate subject-matter already apprehended and crying out for drastic treatment. Every pupil will have concentrated in turn on a variety of different subjects, and will know where his strong points lie. Finally—and this of all the objects to be attained is the most dear to my heart—the science students will have obtained both an invaluable literary education and also at the most impressionable age an early initiation into habits of thinking for themselves in the region of science.

After the age of sixteen new problems arise. For literary students science passes into the stage of generalisation, largely in the form of lectures on its main results and general ideas. New cycles of linguistic, literary, and historical study commence. But further detail is now unnecessary. For the scientists the preceding stage of precision maintains itself to the close of the school period with an increasing apprehension of wider general ideas.

However, at this period of education the problem is too individual, or at least breaks up into too many cases, to be susceptible of broad general treatment. I do suggest, nevertheless, that all scientists should now keep up their French, and initiate the study of German if they have not already acquired it.

University Education

I should now like, if you will bear with me, to make some remarks respecting the import of these ideas for a University education.

The whole period of growth from infancy to manhood forms one grand cycle. Its stage of romance stretches across the first dozen years of life, its stage of precision comprises the whole school period of secondary education, and its stage of generalisation is the period of entrance into manhood. For those whose formal education is prolonged beyond the school age, the University course or its equivalent is the great period of generalisation. The spirit of generalisation should dominate a University. The lectures should be addressed to those to whom details and procedure are familiar; that is to say, familiar at least in the sense of being so congruous to pre-existing training as to be easily acquirable. During the school period the student has been mentally bending over his desk; at the University he should stand up and look around. For this reason it is fatal if the first year at the University be frittered away in going over the old work in the old spirit. At school the boy painfully rises from the particular towards glimpses at general ideas; at the University he should start from general ideas and study their applications to concrete cases. A well-planned University course is a study of the wide sweep of generality. I do not mean that it should be abstract in the sense of divorce from concrete fact, but that concrete fact should be studied as illustrating the scope of general ideas.

Cultivation of Mental Power

This is the aspect of University training in which theoretical interest and practical utility coincide. Whatever be the detail with which you cram your student, the chance of his meeting in after-life exactly that detail is almost infinitesimal; and if he does meet it, he will probably have forgotten what you taught him about it. The really useful training yields a comprehension of a few general principles with a thorough grounding in the way they apply to a variety of concrete details. In subsequent practice the men will have forgotten your particular details; but they will remember by an unconscious common sense how to apply principles to immediate circumstances. Your learning is useless to you till you have lost your text-books, burnt your lecture notes, and forgotten the minutiæ which you learnt by heart for the examination. What, in the way of detail, you continually require will stick in your memory as obvious facts like the sun and moon; and what you casually require can be looked up in any work of reference. The function of a University is to enable you to shed details in favour of principles. When I speak of principles I am hardly even thinking of verbal formulations. A principle which has thoroughly soaked into you is rather a mental habit than a formal statement. It becomes the way the mind reacts to the appropriate stimulus in the form of illustrative circumstances. Nobody goes about with his knowledge clearly and consciously before him.

Mental cultivation is nothing else than the satisfactory way in which the mind will function when it is poked up into activity. Learning is often spoken of as if we are watching the open pages of all the books which we have ever read, and then, when occasion arises, we select the right page to read aloud to the universe.

Luckily, the truth is far otherwise from this crude idea; and for this reason the antagonism between the claims of pure knowledge and professional acquirement should be much less acute than a faulty view of education would lead us to anticipate. I can put my point otherwise by saying that the ideal of a University is not so much knowledge, as power. Its business is to convert the knowledge of a boy into the power of a man.

The Rhythmic Character of Growth

I will conclude with two remarks which I wish to make by way of caution in the interpretation of my meaning. The point of this address is the rhythmic character of growth. The interior spiritual life of man is a web of many strands. They do not all grow together by uniform extension. I have tried to illustrate this truth by considering the normal unfolding of the capacities of a child in somewhat favourable circumstances but otherwise with fair average capacities. Perhaps I have misconstrued the usual phenomena. It is very likely that I have so failed, for the evidence is complex and difficult. But do not let any failure in this respect prejudice the main point which I am here to enforce. It is that the development of mentality exhibits itself as a rhythm involving an interweaving of cycles, the whole process being dominated by a greater cycle of the same general character as its minor eddies. Furthermore, this rhythm exhibits certain ascertainable general laws which are valid for most pupils, and the quality of our teaching should be so adapted as to suit the stage in the rhythm to which our pupils have advanced. The problem of a curriculum is not so much the succession of subjects; for all subjects should in essence be begun with the dawn of mentality. The truly important order is the order of quality which the educational procedure should assume.

My second caution is to ask you not to exaggerate into sharpness the distinction between the three stages of a cycle. I strongly suspect that many of you, when you heard me detail the three stages in each cycle, said to yourselves—How like a mathematician to make such formal divisions! I assure you that it is not mathematics but literary incompetence that may have led me into the error against which I am warning you. Of course, I mean throughout a distinction of emphasis, of pervasive quality—romance, precision, generalisation, are all present throughout. But there is an alternation of dominance, and it is this alternation which constitutes the cycles.

CHAPTER III

The Rhythmic Claims of Freedom and Discipline

The fading of ideals is sad evidence of the defeat of human endeavour. In the schools of antiquity philosophers aspired to impart wisdom, in modern colleges our humbler aim is to teach subjects. The drop from the divine wisdom, which was the goal of the ancients, to text-book knowledge of subjects, which is achieved by the moderns, marks an educational failure, sustained through the ages. I am not maintaining that in the practice of education the ancient were more successful than ourselves. You have only to read Lucian, and to note his satiric dramatizations of the pretentious claims of philosophers, to see that in this respect the ancients can boast over us no superiority. My point is that, at the dawn of our European civilisation, men started with the full ideals which should inspire education, and that gradually our ideals have sunk to square with our practice.

But when ideals have sunk to the level of practice, the result is stagnation. In particular, so long as we conceive intellectual education as merely consisting in the acquirement of mechanical mental aptitudes, and of formulated statements of useful truths, there can be no progress; though there will be much activity, amid aimless re-arrangement of syllabuses, in the fruitless endeavour to dodge the inevitable lack of time. We must take it as an unavoidable fact, that God has so made the world that there are more topics desirable for knowledge than any one person can possibly acquire. It is hopeless to approach the problem by the way of the enumeration of subjects which every one ought to have mastered. There are too many of them, all with excellent title-deeds. Perhaps, after all, this plethora of material is fortunate; for the world is made interesting by a delightful ignorance of important truths. What I am anxious to impress on you is that though knowledge is one chief aim of intellectual education, there is another ingredient, vaguer but greater, and more dominating in its importance. The ancients called it "wisdom." You cannot be wise without some basis of knowledge; but you may easily acquire knowledge and remain bare of wisdom.

Now wisdom is the way in which knowledge is held. It concerns the handling of knowledge, its selection for the determination of relevant issues, its employment to add value to our immediate experience. This mastery of knowledge, which is wisdom, is the most intimate freedom obtainable. The ancients saw clearly—more clearly than we do—the necessity for dominating knowledge by wisdom. But, in the pursuit of wisdom in the region of practical education, they erred sadly. To put the matter simply, their popular practice assumed that wisdom could be imparted to the young by procuring philosophers to spout at them. Hence the crop of shady philosophers in the schools of the ancient world. The only avenue towards wisdom is by freedom in the presence of knowledge. But the only avenue towards knowledge is by discipline in the acquirement of ordered fact. Freedom and discipline are the two essentials of education, and hence the title of my discourse to-day, "The Rhythmic Claims of Freedom and Discipline."

The antithesis in education between freedom and discipline is not so sharp as a logical analysis of the meanings of the terms might lead us to imagine. The pupil's mind is a growing organism. On the one hand, it is not a box to be ruthlessly packed with alien ideas: and, on the other hand, the ordered acquirement of know-ledge is the natural food for a developing intelligence. Accordingly, it should be the aim of an ideally constructed education that the discipline should be the voluntary issue of free choice, and that the freedom should gain an enrichment of possibility as the issue of discipline. The two principles, freedom and discipline, are not antagonists, but should be so adjusted in the child's life that they correspond to a natural sway, to and fro, of the developing personality. It is this adaptation of freedom and discipline to the natural sway of development that I have elsewhere called The Rhythm of Education. I am convinced that much disappointing failure in the past has been due to neglect of attention to the importance of this rhythm. My main position is that the dominant note of education at its beginning and at its end is freedom, but that there is an intermediate stage of discipline with freedom in subordination: Furthermore, that there is not one unique threefold cycle of freedom, discipline, and freedom; but that all mental development is composed of such cycles, and of cycles of such cycles. Such a cycle is a unit cell, or brick; and the complete stage of growth is an organic structure of such cells. In analysing any one such cell, I call the first period of freedom the "stage of Romance," the intermediate period of discipline I call the "stage of Precision," and the final period of freedom is the "stage of Generalisation."

Let me now explain myself in more detail. There can be no mental development without interest. Interest is the *sine qua non* for attention and apprehension. You may endeavour to excite interest by means of birch rods, or you may coax it by the incitement of pleasurable activity. But without interest there will be no progress. Now the natural mode by which living organisms are excited towards suitable self-development is enjoyment. The infant is lured to adapt itself to its environment by its love of its mother and its nurse; we eat because we like a good dinner; we subdue the forces of nature because we have been lured to discovery by an insatiable curiosity: we enjoy exercise: and we enjoy the unchristian passion of hating our dangerous enemies. Undoubtedly pain is one subordinate means of arousing an organism to action. But it only supervenes on the failure of pleasure. Joy is the normal healthy spur for the *élan vital*. I am not maintaining that we can safely abandon ourselves to the allurement of the greater immediate joys. What I do mean is that we should seek to arrange the development of character along a path of natural activity, in itself pleasurable. The subordinate stiffening of discipline must be directed to secure some long-time good; although an adequate object must not be too far below the horizon, if the necessary interest is to be retained.

The second preliminary point which I wish to make, is the

unimportance—indeed the evil—of barren knowledge. The importance of knowledge lies in its use, in our active mastery of it—that is to say, it lies in wisdom. It is a convention to speak of mere knowledge, apart from wisdom, as of itself imparting a peculiar dignity to its possessor. I do not share in this reverence for knowledge as such. It all depends on who has the knowledge and what he does with it. That knowledge which adds greatness to character is knowledge so handled as to transform every phase of immediate experience. It is in respect to the activity of knowledge that an over-vigorous discipline in education is so harmful. The habit of active thought, with freshness, can only be generated by adequate freedom. Undiscriminating discipline defeats its own object by dulling the mind. If you have much to do with the young as they emerge from school and from the university, you soon note the dulled minds of those whose education has consisted in the acquirement of inert knowledge. Also the deplorable tone of English society in respect to learning is a tribute to our educational failure. Furthermore, this overhaste to impart mere knowledge defeats itself. The human mind rejects knowledge imparted in this way. The craving for expansion, for activity, inherent in youth is disgusted by a dry imposition of disciplined knowledge. The discipline, when it comes, should satisfy a natural craving for the wisdom which adds value to bare experience.

But let us now examine more closely the rhythm of these natural cravings of the human intelligence. The first procedure of the mind in a new environment is a somewhat discursive activity amid a welter of ideas and experience. It is a process of discovery, a process of becoming used to curious thoughts, of shaping questions, of seeking for answers, of devising new experiences, of noticing what happens as the result of new ventures. This general process is both natural and of absorbing interest. We must often have noticed children between the ages of eight and thirteen absorbed in its ferment. It is dominated by wonder, and cursed be the dullard who destroys wonder. Now undoubtedly this stage of development requires help, and even discipline. The environment within which the mind is working must be carefully selected. It must, of course, be chosen to suit the child's stage of growth, and must be adapted to individual needs. In a sense it is an imposition from without;

but in a deeper sense it answers to the call of life within the child. In the teacher's consciousness the child has been sent to his telescope to look at the stars, in the child's consciousness he has been given free access to the glory of the heavens. Unless, working somewhere, however obscurely, even in the dullest child, there is this transfiguration of imposd routine, the child's nature will refuse to assimilate the alien material. It must never be forgotten that education is not a process of packing articles in a trunk. Such a simile is entirely inapplicable. It is, of course, a process completely of its own peculiar genus. Its nearest analogue is the assimilation of food by a living organism: and we all know how necessary to health is palatable food under suitable conditions. When you have put your boots in a trunk, they will stay there till you take them out again; but this is not at all the case if you feed a child with the wrong food.

This initial stage of romance requires guidance in another way. After all the child is the heir to long ages of civilisation, and it is absurd to let him wander in the intellectual maze of men in the Glacial Epoch. Accordingly, a certain pointing out of important facts, and of simplifying ideas, and of usual names, really strengthens the natural impetus of the pupil. In no part of education can you do without discipline or can you do without freedom; but in the stage of romance the emphasis must always be on freedom, to allow the child to see for itself and to act for itself. My point is that a block in the assimilation of ideas inevitably arises when a discipline of precision is imposed before a stage of romance has run its course in the growing mind. There is no comprehension apart from romance. It is my strong belief that the cause of so much failure in the past has been due to the lack of careful study of the due place of romance. Without the adventure of romance, at the best you get inert knowledge without initiative, and at the worst you get contempt of ideas—without knowledge.

But when this stage of romance has been properly guided another craving grows. The freshness of inexperience has worn off; there is general knowledge of the groundwork of fact and theory: and, above all, there has been plenty of independent browsing amid first-hand experiences, involving adventures of thought and of action. The enlightenment which comes from precise knowledge can now be understood. It corresponds to the obvious requirements of common sense, and deals with familiar material. Now is the time for pushing on, for knowing the subject exactly, and for retaining in the memory its salient features. This is the stage of precision. This stage is the sole stage of learning in the traditional scheme of education, either at school or university. You had to learn your subject, and there was nothing more to be said on the topic of education. The result of such an undue extension of a most necessary period of development was the production of a plentiful array of dunces, and of a few scholars whose natural interest had survived the car of Juggernaut. There is, indeed, always the temptation to teach pupils a little more of fact and of precise theory than at that stage they are fitted to assimilate. If only they could, it would be so useful. We—I am talking of schoolmasters and of university dons— are apt to forget that we are only subordinate elements in the education of a grown man; and that, in their own good time, in later life our pupils will learn for themselves. The phenomena of growth cannot be hurried beyond certain very narrow limits. But an unskilful practitioner can easily damage a sensitive organism. Yet, when all has been said in the way of caution, there is such a thing as pushing on, of getting to know the fundamental details and the main exact generalisations, and of acquiring an easy mastery of technique. There is no getting away from the fact that things have been found out, and that to be effective in the modern world you must have a store of definite acquirement of the best practice. To write poetry you must study metre; and to build bridges you must be learned in the strength of material. Even the Hebrew prophets had learned to write, probably in those days requiring no mean effort. The untutored art of genius is—in the words of the Prayer Book—a vain thing, fondly invented.

During the stage of precision, romance is the background. The stage is dominated by the inescapable fact that there are right ways and wrong ways, and definite truths to be known. But romance is not dead, and it is the art of teaching to foster it amidst definite application to appointed task. It must be fostered for one reason, because romance is after all a necessary ingredient of that balanced wisdom which is the goal to be attained. But there is another reason: The organism will not absorb the fruits of the task unless its powers of apprehension are kept fresh by romance. The real point is to discover in practice that exact balance between freedom and discipline which will give the greatest rate of progress over the things to be known. I do not believe that there is any abstract formula which will give information applicable to all subjects, to all types of pupils, or to each individual pupil; except indeed the formula of rhythmic sway which I have been insisting on, namely, that in the earlier stage the progress requires that the emphasis be laid on freedom, and that in the later middle stage the emphasis be laid on the definite acquirement of allotted tasks. I freely admit that if the stage of romance has been properly managed, the discipline of the second stage is much less apparent, that the children know how to go about their work, want to make a good job of it, and can be safely trusted with the details. Furthermore, I hold that the only discipline, important for its own sake, is self-discipline, and that this can only be acquired by a wide use of freedom. But yet—so many are the delicate points to be considered in education—it is necessary in life to have acquired the habit of cheerfully undertaking imposed tasks. The conditions can be satisfied if the tasks correspond to the natural cravings of the pupil at his stage of progress, if they keep his powers at full stretch, and if they attain an obviously sensible result, and if reasonable freedom is allowed in the mode of execution.

The difficulty of speaking about the way a skilful teacher will keep romance alive in his pupils arises from the fact that what takes a long time to describe, takes a short time to do. The beauty of a passage of Virgil may be rendered by insisting on beauty of verbal enunciation, taking no longer than prosy utterance. The emphasis on the beauty of a mathematical argument, in its marshalling of general considerations to unravel complex fact, is the speediest mode of procedure. The responsibility of the teacher at this stage is immense. To speak the truth, except in the rare case of genius in the teacher, I do not think that it is possible to take a whole class very far along the road of precision without some dulling of the interest. It is the unfortunate dilemma that initiative and training are both necessary, and that training is apt to kill initiative.

But this admission is not to condone a brutal ignorance of methods of mitigating this untoward fact. It is not a theoretical necessity, but arises because perfect tact is unattainable in the treatment of each individual case. In the past the methods employed assassinated interest; we are discussing how to reduce the evil to its smallest dimensions. I merely utter the warning that education is a difficult problem, to be solved by no one simple formula.

In this connection there is, however, one practical consideration which is largely neglected. The territory of romantic interest is large, ill-defined, and not to be controlled by any explicit boundary. It depends on the chance flashes of insight. But the area of precise knowledge, as exacted in any general educational system, can be, and should be, definitely determined. If you make it too wide you will kill interest and defeat your own object: if you make it too narrow your pupils will lack effective grip. Surely, in every subject in each type of curriculum, the precise knowledge required should be determined after the most anxious inquiry. This does not now seem to be the case in any effective way. For example, in the classical studies of boys destined for a scientific career—a class of pupils in whom I am greatly interested—What is the Latin vocabulary which they ought definitely to know? Also what are the grammatical rules and constructions which they ought to have mastered? Why not determine these once and for all, and then bend every exercise to impress just these on the memory, and to understand their derivatives, both in Latin and also in French and English. Then, as to other constructions and words which occur in the reading of texts, supply full information in the easiest manner. A certain ruthless definiteness is essential in education. I am sure that one secret of a successful teacher is that he has formulated quite clearly in his mind what the pupil has got to know in precise fashion. He will then cease from half-hearted attempts to worry his pupils with memorising a lot of irrelevant stuff of inferior importance. The secret of success is pace, and the secret of pace is concentration. But, in respect to precise knowledge, the watchword is pace, pace, pace. Get your knowledge quickly, and then use it. If you can use it, you will retain it.

We have now come to the third stage of the rhythmic cycle, the stage of generalisation. There is here a reaction towards romance. Something definite is now known; aptitudes have been acquired; and general rules and laws are clearly apprehended both in their formulation and their detailed exemplification. The pupil now wants to use his new weapons. He is an effective individual, and it is effects that he wants to produce. He relapses into the discursive adventures of the romantic stage, with the advantage that his mind is now a disciplined regiment instead of a rabble. In this sense, education should begin in research and end in research. After all, the whole affair is merely a preparation for battling with the immediate experiences of life, a preparation by which to qualify each immediate moment with relevant ideas and appropriate actions. An education which does not begin by evoking initiative and end by encouraging it must be wrong. For its whole aim is the production of active wisdom.

In my own work at universities I have been much struck by the paralysis of thought induced in pupils by the aimless accumulation of precise knowledge, inert and unutilised. It should be the chief aim of a university professor to exhibit himself in his own true character—that is, as an ignorant man thinking, actively utilising his small share of knowledge. In a sense, knowledge shrinks as wisdom grows: for details are swallowed up in principles. The details of knowledge which are important will be picked up *ad hoc* in each avocation of life, but the habit of the active utilisation of well-understood principles is the final possession of wisdom. The stage of precision is the stage of growing into the apprehension of principles by the acquisition of a precise knowledge of details. The stage of generalisations is the stage of shedding details in favour of the active application of principles, the details retreating into subconscious habits. We don't go about explicitly retaining in our own minds that two and two make four, though once we had to learn it by heart. We trust to habit for our elementary arithmetic. But the essence of this stage is the emergence from the comparative passivity of being trained into the active freedom of application. Of course, during this stage, precise knowledge will grow, and more actively than ever before, because the mind has experienced the power of definiteness, and responds to the acquisition of general truth, and of richness of illustration. But the growth of knowledge becomes progressively unconscious, as being an incident derived from some active adventure of thought.

So much for the three stages of the rhythmic unit of development. In a general way the whole period of education is dominated by this threefold rhythm. Till the age of thirteen or fourteen there is the romantic stage, from fourteen to eighteen the stage of precision, and from eighteen to two and twenty the stage of generalisation. But these are only average characters, tinging the mode of development as a whole. I do not think that any pupil completes his stages simultaneously in all subjects. For example, I should plead that while language is initiating its stage of precision in the way of acquisition of vocabulary and of grammar, science should be in its full romantic stage. The romantic stage of language begins in infancy with the acquisition of speech, so that it passes early towards a stage of precision; while science is a late comer. Accordingly a precise inculcation of science at an early age wipes out initiative and interest, and destroys any chance of the topic having any richness of content in the child's apprehension. Thus, the romantic stage of science should persist for years after the precise study of language has commenced.

There are minor eddies, each in itself a threefold cycle, running its course in each day, in each week, and in each term. There is the general apprehension of some topic in its vague possibilities, the mastery of the relevant details, and finally the putting of the whole subject together in the light of the relevant knowledge. Unless the pupils are continually sustained by the evocation of interest, the acquirement of technique, and the excitement of success, they can never make progress, and will certainly lose heart. Speaking generally, during the last thirty years the schools of England have been sending up to the universities a disheartened crowd of young folk, inoculated against any outbreak of intellectual zeal. The universities have seconded the efforts of the schools and emphasised the failure. Accordingly, the cheerful gaiety of the young turns to other topics, and thus educated England is not hospitable to ideas. When we can point to some great achievement of our nation—let us hope that it may be something other than a war—which has been won in the class-room of our schools, and not in their playing-fields, then we may feel content with our modes of education.

So far I have been discussing intellectual education, and my argument has been cramped on too narrow a basis. After all, our pupils are alive, and cannot be chopped into separate bits, like the pieces of a jig-saw puzzle. In the production of a mechanism the constructive energy lies outside it, and adds discrete parts to discrete parts. The case is far different for a living organism which grows by its own impulse towards self-development. This impulse can be stimulated and guided from outside the organism, and it can also be killed. But for all your stimulation and guidance the creative impulse towards growth comes from within, and is intensely characteristic of the individual. Education is the guidance of the individual towards a comprehension of the art of life; and by the art of life I mean the most complete achievement of varied activity expressing the potentialities of that living creature in the face of its actual environment. This completeness of achievement involves an artistic sense, subordinating the lower to the higher possibilities of the indivisible personality. Science, art, religion, morality, take their rise from this sense of values within the structure of being. Each individual embodies an adventure of existence. The art of life is the guidance of this adventure. The great religions of civilisation include among their original elements revolts against the inculcation of morals as a set of isolated prohibitions. Morality, in the petty negative sense of the term, is the deadly enemy of religion. Paul denounces the Law, and the Gospels are vehement against the Pharisees. Every outbreak of religion exhibits the same intensity of antagonism—an antagonism diminishing as religion fades. No part of education has more to gain from attention to the rhythmic law of growth than has moral and religious education. Whatever be the right way to formulate religious truths, it is death to religion to insist on a premature stage of precision. The vitality of religion is shown by the way in which the religious spirit has survived the ordeal of religious education.

The problem of religion in education is too large to be discussed at this stage of my address. I have referred to it to guard against the suspicion that the principles here advocated are to be conceived in a narrow sense. We are analysing the general law of rhythmic progress in the higher stages of life, embodying the initial awakening, the discipline, and the fruition on the higher plane. What I am now insisting is that the principle of progress is from within: the discovery is made by ourselves, the discipline is self-discipline, and the fruition is the outcome of our own initiative. The teacher has a double function. It is for him to elicit the enthusiasm by resonance from his own personality, and to create the environment of a larger knowledge and a firmer purpose. He is there to avoid the waste, which in the lower stages of existence is nature's way of evolution. The ultimate motive power, alike in science, in morality, and in religion, is the sense of value, the sense of importance. It takes the various forms of wonder, of curiosity, of reverence, or worship, of tumultuous desire for merging personality in something beyond itself. This sense of value imposes on life incredible labours, and apart from it life sinks back into the passivity of its lower types. The most penetrating exhibition of this force is the sense of beauty, the æsthetic sense of realised perfection. This thought leads me to ask, whether in our modern education we emphasise sufficiently the functions of art.

The typical education of our public schools was devised for boys from well-to-do cultivated homes. They travelled in Italy, in Greece, and in France, and often their own homes were set amid beauty. None of these circumstances hold for modern national education in primary or secondary schools, or even for the majority of boys and girls in our enlarged system of public schools. You cannot, without loss, ignore in the life of the spirit so great a factor as art. Our æsthetic emotions provide us with vivid apprehensions of value. If you maim these, you weaken the force of the whole system of spiritual apprehensions. The claim for freedom in education carries with it the corollary that the development of the whole personality must be attended to. You must not arbitrarily refuse its urgent demands. In these days of economy, we hear much of the futility of our educational efforts and of the possibility of curtailing them. The endeavour to develop a bare intellectuality is bound to issue in a large crop of failure. This is just what we have done in our national schools. We do just enough to excite and not enough to satisfy. History shows us that an efflorescence of art is the first activity of nations on the road to civilisation. Yet, in the face of this plain fact, we practically shut out art from the masses of the population. Can we wonder that such an education, evoking and defeating cravings, leads to failure and discontent? The stupidity of the whole procedure is, that art in simple popular forms is just what we can give to the nation without undue strain on our resources. You may, perhaps, by some great reforms, obviate the worse kind of sweated labour and the insecurity of employment. But you can never greatly increase average incomes. On that side all hope of Utopia is closed to you. It would, however, require no very great effort to use our schools to produce a population with some love of music, some enjoyment of drama, and some joy in beauty of form and colour. We could also provide means for the satisfaction of these emotions in the general life of the population. If you think of the simplest ways, you will see that the strain on material resources would be negligible; and when you have done that, and when your population widely appreciates what art can give—its joys and its terrors—do you not think that your prophets and your clergy and your statesmen will be in a stronger position when they speak to the population of the love of God, of the inexorableness of duty, and of the call of patriotism?

Shakespeare wrote his plays for English people reared in the beauty of the country, amid the pageant of life as the Middle Age merged into the Renaissance, and with a new world across the ocean to make vivid the call of romance. To-day we deal with herded town populations, reared in a scientific age. I have no doubt that unless we can meet the new age with new methods, to sustain for our populations the life of the spirit, sooner or later, amid some savage outbreak of defeated longings, the fate of Russia will be the fate of England. Historians will write as her epitaph that her fall issued from the spiritual blindness of her governing classes, from their dull materialism, and from their Pharisaic attachment to petty formulæ of statesmanship.

CHAPTER IV

Technical Education and Its Relation to Science and Literature

The subject of this address is Technical Education. I wish to examine its essential nature and also its relation to a liberal education. Such an inquiry may help us to realise the conditions for the successful working of a national system of technical training. It is also a very burning question among mathematical teachers; for mathematics is included in most technological courses.

Now it is unpractical to plunge into such a discussion without framing in our own minds the best ideal towards which we desire to work, however modestly we may frame our hopes as to the result which in the near future is likely to be achieved.

People are shy of ideals; and accordingly we find a formulation of the ideal state of mankind placed by a modern dramatist[1] in the mouth of a mad priest: "In my dreams it is a country where the State is the Church and the Church the people: three in one and one in three. It is a commonwealth in which work is play and play is life: three in one and one in three. It is a temple in which the priest is the worshipper and the worshipper the worshipped: three in one and one in three. It is a godhead in which all life is human and all humanity divine: three in one and one in three. It is, in short, the dream of a madman."

Now the part of this speech to which I would direct attention is embodied in the phrase, "It is a commonwealth in which work is

[1] Cf. BERNARD SHAW: *John Bull's Other Island.*

play and play is life." This is the ideal of technical education. It sounds very mystical when we confront it with the actual facts, the toiling millions, tired, discontented, mentally indifferent, and then the employers—I am not undertaking a social analysis, but I shall carry you with me when I admit that the present facts of society are a long way off this ideal. Furthermore, we are agreed that an employer who conducted his workshop on the principle that "work should be play" would be ruined in a week.

The curse that has been laid on humanity, in fable and in fact, is, that by the sweat of its brow shall it live. But reason and moral intuition have seen in this curse the foundation for advance. The early Benedictine monks rejoiced in their labours because they conceived themselves as thereby made fellow-workers with Christ.

Stripped of its theological trappings, the essential idea remains, that work should be transfused with intellectual and moral vision and thereby turned into a joy, triumphing over its weariness and its pain. Each of us will re-state this abstract formulation in a more concrete shape in accordance with his private outlook. State it how you like, so long as you do not lose the main point in your details. However you phrase it, it remains the sole real hope of toiling humanity; and it is in the hands of technical teachers, and of those who control their spheres of activity, so to mould the nation that daily it may pass to its labours in the spirit of the monks of old.

The immediate need of the nation is a large supply of skilled workmen, of men with inventive genius, and of employers alert in the development of new ideas.

There is one—and only one—way to obtain these admirable results. It is by producing workmen, men of science, and employers who enjoy their work. View the matter practically in the light of our knowledge of average human nature. Is it likely that a tired, bored workman, however skilful his hands, will produce a large output of first-class work? He will limit his production, will scamp his work, and be an adept at evading inspection; he will be slow in adapting himself to new methods; he will be a focus of discontent, full of unpractical revolutionary ideas, controlled by no sympathetic apprehension of the real working of trade conditions. If, in the troubled times which may be before us, you wish appreciably to increase the chance of some savage upheaval, introduce widespread technical education and ignore the Benedictine ideal. Society will then get what it deserves.

Again, inventive genius requires pleasurable mental activity as a condition for its vigorous exercise. "Necessity is the mother of invention" is a silly proverb. "Necessity is the mother of futile dodges" is much nearer to the truth. The basis of the growth of modern invention is science, and science is almost wholly the outgrowth of pleasurable intellectual curiosity.

The third class are the employers, who are to be enterprising. Now it is to be observed that it is the successful employers who are the important people to get at, the men with business connections all over the world, men who are already rich. No doubt there will always be a continuous process of rise and fall of businesses. But it is futile to expect flourishing trade, if in the mass the successful houses of business are suffering from atrophy. Now if these men conceive their businesses as merely indifferent means for acquiring other disconnected opportunities of life, they have no spur to alertness. They are already doing very well, the mere momentum of their present business engagements will carry them on for their time. They are not at all likely to bother themselves with the doubtful chances of new methods. Their real soul is in the other side of their life. Desire for money will produce hard-fistedness and not enterprise. There is much more hope for humanity from manufacturers who enjoy their work than from those who continue in irksome business with the object of founding hospitals.

Finally, there can be no prospect of industrial peace so long as masters and men in the mass conceive themselves as engaged in a soulless operation of extracting money from the public. Enlarged views of the work performed, and of the communal service thereby rendered, can be the only basis on which to found sympathetic co-operation.

The conclusion to be drawn from this discussion is, that alike for masters and for men a technical or technological education, which is to have any chance of satisfying the practical needs of the nation, must be conceived in a liberal spirit as a real intellectual enlightenment in regard to principles applied and services rendered. In such an education geometry and poetry are as essential as turning laths.

The mythical figure of Plato may stand for modern liberal education as does that of St. Benedict for technical education. We need not entangle ourselves in the qualifications necessary for a balanced representation of the actual thoughts of the actual men. They are used here as symbolic figures typical of antithetical notions. We consider Plato in the light of the type of culture he now inspires.

In its essence a liberal education is an education for thought and for æsthetic appreciation. It proceeds by imparting a knowledge of the masterpieces of thought, of imaginative literature, and of art. The action which it contemplates is command. It is an aristocratic education implying leisure. This Platonic ideal has rendered imperishable services to European civilisation. It has encouraged art, it has fostered that spirit of disinterested curiosity which is the origin of science, it has maintained the dignity of mind in the face of material force, a dignity which claims freedom of thought. Plato did not, like St. Benedict, bother himself to be a fellow-worker with his slaves; but he must rank among the emancipators of mankind. His type of culture is the peculiar inspiration of the liberal aristocrat, the class from which Europe derives what ordered liberty it now possesses. For centuries, from Pope Nicholas V to the school of the Jesuits, and from the Jesuits to the modern headmasters of English public schools, this educational ideal has had the strenuous support of the clergy.

For certain people it is a very good education. It suits their type of mind and the circumstances amid which their life is passed. But more has been claimed for it than this. All education has been judged adequate or defective according to its approximation to this sole type.

The essence of the type is a large discursive knowledge of the best literature. The ideal product of the type is the man who is acquainted with the best that has been written. He will have acquired the chief languages, he will have considered the histories of the rise and fall of nations, the poetic expression of human feeling, and have read the great dramas and novels. He will also be well grounded in the chief philosophies, and have attentively read those philosophic authors who are distinguished for lucidity of style.

It is obvious that, except at the close of a long life, he will not have much time for anything else if any approximation is to be made to the fulfilment of this programme. One is reminded of the calculation in a dialogue of Lucian that, before a man could be justified in practising any one of the current ethical systems, he should have spent a hundred and fifty years in examining their credentials.

Such ideals are not for human beings. What is meant by a liberal culture is nothing so ambitious as a full acquaintance with the varied literary expression of civilised mankind from Asia to Europe, and from Europe to America. A small selection only is required; but then, as we are told, it is a selection of the very best. I have my doubts of a selection which includes Xenophon and omits Confucius, but then I have read through neither in the original. The ambitious programme of a liberal education really shrinks to a study of some fragments of literature included in a couple of important languages.

But the expression of the human spirit is not confined to literature. There are the other arts, and there are the sciences. Also education must pass beyond the passive reception of the ideas of others. Powers of initiative must be strengthened. Unfortunately initiative does not mean just one acquirement—there is initiative in thought, initiative in action, and the imaginative initiative of art; and these three categories require many subdivisions.

The field of acquirement is large, and the individual so fleeting and so fragmentary: classical scholars, scientists, headmasters are alike ignoramuses.

There is a curious illusion that a more complete culture was possible when there was less to know. Surely the only gain was, that it was more possible to remain unconscious of ignorance. It cannot have been a gain to Plato to have read neither Shakespeare, nor Newton, nor Darwin. The achievements of a liberal education have in recent times not been worsened. The change is that its pretensions have been found out.

My point is, that no course of study can claim any position of ideal completeness. Nor are the omitted factors of subordinate importance. The insistence in the Platonic culture on disinterested intellectual appreciation is a psychological error. Action and our implication in the transition of events amid the inevitable bond of cause to effect are fundamental. An education which strives to divorce intellectual or æsthetic life from these fundamental facts carries with it the decadence of civilisation. Essentially culture should be for action, and its effect should be to divest labour from the associations of aimless toil. Art exists that we may know the deliverances of our senses as good. It heightens the sense-world.

Disinterested scientific curiosity is a passion for an ordered intellectual vision of the connection of events. But the goal of such curiosity is the marriage of action to thought. This essential intervention of action even in abstract science is often overlooked. No man of science wants merely to know. He acquires knowledge to appease his passion for discovery. He does not discover in order to know, he knows in order to discover. The pleasure which art and science can give to toil is the enjoyment which arises from successfully directed intention. Also it is the same pleasure which is yielded to the scientist and to the artist.

The antithesis between a technical and a liberal education is fallacious. There can be no adequate technical education which is not liberal, and no liberal education which is not technical: that is, no education which does not impart both technique and intellectual vision. In simpler language, education should turn out the pupil with something he knows well and something he can do well. This intimate union of practice and theory aids both. The intellect does not work best in a vacuum. The stimulation of creative impulse requires, especially in the case of a child, the quick transition to practice. Geometry and mechanics, followed by workshop practice, gain that reality without which mathematics is verbiage.

There are three main methods which are required in a national system of education, namely, the literary curriculum, the scientific curriculum, the technical curriculum. But each of these curricula should include the other two. What I mean is, that every form of education should give the pupil a technique, a science, an assortment of general ideas, and æsthetic appreciation, and that each of these sides of his training should be illuminated by the others. Lack of time, even for the most favoured pupil, makes it impossible to develop fully each curriculum. Always there must be a dominant emphasis. The most direct æsthetic training naturally falls in the technical curriculum in those cases when the training is that requisite for some art or artistic craft. But it is of high importance in both a literary and a scientific education.

The educational method of the literary curriculum is the study of language, that is, the study of our most habitual method of conveying to others our states of mind. The technique which should be acquired is the technique of verbal expression, the science is the study of the structure of language and the analysis of the relations of language to the states of mind conveyed. Furthermore, the subtle relations of language to feeling, and the high development of the sense organs to which written and spoken words appeal, lead to keen æsthetic appreciations being aroused by the successful employment of language. Finally, the wisdom of the world is preserved in the masterpieces of linguistic composition.

This curriculum has the merit of homogeneity. All its various parts are co-ordinated and play into each other's hands. We can hardly be surprised that such a curriculum, when once broadly established, should have claimed the position of the sole perfect type of education. Its defect is unduly to emphasise the importance of language. Indeed the varied importance of verbal expression is so overwhelming that its sober estimation is difficult. Recent generations have been witnessing the retreat of literature, and of literary forms of expression, from their position of unique importance in intellectual life. In order truly to become a servant and a minister of nature something more is required than literary aptitudes.

A scientific education is primarily a training in the art of observing natural phenomena, and in the knowledge and deduction of laws concerning the sequence of such phenomena. But here, as in the case of a liberal education, we are met by the limitations imposed by shortness of time. There are many types of natural phenomena, and to each type there corresponds a science with its peculiar modes of observation, and its peculiar types of thought employed in the deduction of laws. A study of science in general is impossible in education, all that can be achieved is the study of two or three allied sciences. Hence the charge of narrow specialism urged against any education which is primarily scientific. It is obvious that the charge is apt to be well-founded; and it is worth considering how, within the limits of a scientific education and to the advantage of such an education, the danger can be avoided.

Such a discussion requires the consideration of technical education. A technical education is in the main a training in the art of utilising knowledge for the manufacture of material products. Such a training emphasises manual skill, and the co-ordinated action of hand and eye, and judgment in the control of the process of construction. But judgment necessitates knowledge of those natural processes of which the manufacture is the utilisation. Thus somewhere in technical training an education in scientific knowledge is required. If you minimise the scientific side, you will confine it to the scientific experts; if you maximise it, you will impart it in some measure to the men, and—what is of no less importance—to the directors and managers of the businesses.

Technical education is not necessarily allied exclusively to science on its mental side. It may be an education for an artist or for apprentices to an artistic craft. In that case æsthetic appreciation will have to be cultivated in connection with it.

An evil side of the Platonic culture has been its total neglect of technical education as an ingredient in the complete development of ideal human beings. This neglect has arisen from two disastrous antitheses, namely, that between mind and body, and that between thought and action. I will here interject, solely to avoid criticism, that I am well aware that the Greeks highly valued physical beauty and physical activity. They had, however, that perverted sense of values which is the nemesis of slave-owning.

I lay it down as an educational axiom that in teaching you will come to grief as soon as you forget that your pupils have bodies. This is exactly the mistake of the post-renaissance Platonic curriculum. But nature can be kept at bay by no pitchfork; so in English education, being expelled from the class-room, she returned with a cap and bells in the form of all-conquering athleticism.

The connections between intellectual activity and the body, though diffused in every bodily feeling, are focussed in the eyes, the ears, the voice, and the hands. There is a co-ordination of senses and thought, and also a reciprocal influence between brain activity and material creative activity. In this reaction the hands are peculiarly important. It is a moot point whether the human hand created the human brain, or the brain created the hand. Certainly the connection is intimate and reciprocal. Such deep-seated relations are not widely atrophied by a few hundred years of disuse in exceptional families.

The disuse of hand-craft is a contributory cause to the brain-lethargy of aristocracies, which is only mitigated by sport where the concurrent brain-activity is reduced to a minimum and the hand-craft lacks subtlety. The necessity for constant writing and vocal exposition is some slight stimulus to the thought-power of the professional classes. Great readers, who exclude other activities, are not distinguished by subtlety of brain. They tend to be timid conventional thinkers. No doubt this is partly due to their excessive knowledge outrunning their powers of thought; but it is partly due to the lack of brain-stimulus from the productive activities of hand or voice.

In estimating the importance of technical education we must rise above the exclusive association of learning with book-learning. First-hand knowledge is the ultimate basis of intellectual life. To a large extent book-learning conveys second-hand information, and as such can never rise to the importance of immediate practice. Our goal is to see the immediate events of our lives as instances of our general ideas. What the learned world tends to offer is one second-hand scrap of information illustrating ideas derived from another second-hand scrap of information. The second-handedness of the learned world is the secret of its mediocrity. It is tame because it has never been scared by facts. The main importance of Francis Bacon's influence does not lie in any peculiar theory of inductive reasoning which he happened to express, but in the revolt against second-hand information of which he was a leader.

The peculiar merit of a scientific education should be, that it bases thought upon first-hand observation; and the corresponding merit of a technical education is, that it follows our deep natural instinct to translate thought into manual skill, and manual activity into thought.

The thought which science evokes is logical thought. Now logic is of two kinds: the logic of discovery and the logic of the discovered.

The logic of discovery consists in the weighing of probabilities, in discarding details deemed to be irrelevant, in divining the general rules according to which events occur, and in testing hypotheses by devising suitable experiments. This is inductive logic.

The logic of the discovered is the deduction of the special events which, under certain circumstances, would happen in obedience to the assumed laws of nature. Thus when the laws are discovered or assumed, their utilisation entirely depends on deductive logic. Without deductive logic science would be entirely useless. It is merely a barren game to ascend from the particular to the general, unless afterwards we can reverse the process and descend from the general to the particular, ascending and descending like the angels on Jacob's ladder. When Newton had divined the law of gravitation he at once proceeded to calculate the earth's attractions on an apple at its surface and on the moon. We may note in passing that inductive logic would be impossible without deductive logic. Thus Newton's calculations were an essential step in his inductive verification of the great law.

Now mathematics is nothing else than the more complicated parts of the art of deductive reasoning, especially where it concerns number, quantity, and space.

In the teaching of science, the art of thought should be taught: namely, the art of forming clear conceptions applying to first-hand experience, the art of divining the general truths which apply, the art of testing divinations, and the art of utilising general truths by reasoning to more particular cases of some peculiar importance. Furthermore, a power of scientific exposition is necessary, so that the relevant issues from a confused mass of ideas can be stated clearly, with due emphasis on important points.

By the time a science, or a small group of sciences, has been taught thus amply, with due regard to the general art of thought, we have gone a long way towards correcting the specialism of science. The worst of a scientific education based, as necessarily must be the case, on one or two particular branches of science, is that the teachers under the influence of the examination system are apt merely to stuff their pupils with the narrow results of these special sciences. It is essential that the generality of the method be continually brought to light and contrasted with the speciality of the particular application. A man who only knows his own science, as a routine peculiar to that science, does not even know that. He has no fertility of thought, no power of quickly seizing the bearing of alien ideas. He will discover nothing, and be stupid in practical applications.

This exhibition of the general in the particular is extremely difficult to effect, especially in the case of younger pupils. The art of education is never easy. To surmount its difficulties, especially those of elementary education, is a task worthy of the highest genius. It is the training of human souls.

Mathematics, well taught, should be the most powerful instrument in gradually implanting this generality of idea. The essence of mathematics is perpetually to be discarding more special ideas in favour of more general ideas, and special methods in favour of general methods. We express the conditions of a special problem in the form of an equation, but that equation will serve for a hundred other problems, scattered through diverse sciences. The general reasoning is always the powerful reasoning, because deductive cogency is the property of abstract form.

Here, again, we must be careful. We shall ruin mathematical education if we use it merely to impress general truths. The general ideas are the means of connecting particular results. After all, it is the concrete special cases which are important. Thus in the handling of mathematics in your results you cannot be too concrete, and in your methods you cannot be too general. The essential course of reasoning is to generalise what is particular, and then to particularise what is general. Without generality there is no reasoning, without concreteness there is no importance.

Concreteness is the strength of technical education. I would remind you that truths which lack the highest generality are not necessarily concrete facts. For example, $x+y=y+x$ is an algebraic truth more general than $2+2=4$. But "two and two make four" is itself a highly general proposition lacking any element of concreteness. To obtain a concrete proposition immediate intuition of a truth concerning particular objects is requisite; for example, "these two apples and those apples together make four apples" is a concrete proposition, if you have direct perception or immediate memory of the apples.

In order to obtain the full realisation of truths as applying, and not as empty formulæ, there is no alternative to technical education. Mere passive observation is not sufficient. In creation only is there vivid insight into the properties of the object thereby produced. If you want to understand anything, make it yourself, is a sound rule. Your faculties will be alive, your thoughts gain vividness by an immediate translation into acts. Your ideas gain that reality which comes from seeing the limits of their application.

In elementary education this doctrine has long been put into practice. Young children are taught to familiarise themselves with shapes and colours by simple manual operations of cutting out and of sorting. But good though this is, it is not quite what I mean. That is practical experience before you think, experience antecedent to thought in order to create ideas, a very excellent discipline. But technical education should be much more than that: it is creative experience while you think, experience which realises your thought, experience which teaches you to co-ordinate act and thought, experience leading you to associate thought with fore- sight and foresight with achievement. Technical education gives theory, and a shrewd insight as to where theory fails.

A technical education is not to be conceived as a maimed alterna- tive to the perfect Platonic culture: namely, as a defective training unfortunately made necessary by cramped conditions of life. No human being can attain to anything but fragmentary knowledge and a fragmentary training of his capacities. There are, however, three main roads along which we can proceed with good hope of advancing towards the best balance of intellect and character: these are the way of literary culture, the way of scientific culture, the way of technical culture. No one of these methods can be exclusively followed without grave loss of intellectual activity and of character. But a mere mechanical mixture of the three curricula will produce bad results in the shape of scraps of information never inter- connected or utilised. We have already noted as one of the strong points of the traditional literary culture that all its parts are co-ordinated. The problem of education is to retain the dominant emphasis, whether literary, scientific or technical, and without loss of co-ordination to infuse into each way of education something of the other two.

To make definite the problem of technical education fix attention on two ages: one thirteen, when elementary education ends; and the other seventeen, when technical education ends so far as it is compressed within a school curriculum. I am aware that for artisans in junior technical schools a three-years' course would be more usual. On the other hand, for naval officers, and for directing classes generally, a longer time can be afforded. We want to consider the principles to govern a curriculum which shall land these children at the age of seventeen in the position of having technical skill useful to the community.

Their technical manual training should start at thirteen, bearing a modest proportion to the rest of their work, and should increase in each year finally to attain to a substantial proportion. Above all things it should not be too specialised. Workshop finish and workshop dodges, adapted to one particular job, should be taught in the commercial workshop, and should form no essential part of the school course. A properly trained worker would pick them up in no time. In all education the main cause of failure is staleness. Technical education is doomed if we conceive it as a system for catching children young and for giving them one highly specialised manual aptitude. The nation has need of a fluidity of labour, not merely from place to place, but also within reasonable limits of allied aptitudes, from one special type of work to another special type. I know that here I am on delicate ground, and I am not claiming that men while they are specialising on one sort of work should spasmodically be set to other kinds. That is a question of trade organisation with which educationalists have no concern. I am only asserting the principles that training should be broader than the ultimate specialisation, and that the resulting power of adaptation to varying demands is advantageous to the workers, to the employers, and to the nation.

In considering the intellectual side of the curriculum we must be guided by the principle of the co-ordination of studies. In general, the intellectual studies most immediately related to manual training will be some branches of science. More than one branch will, in fact, be concerned; and even if that be not the case, it is impossible to narrow down scientific study to a single thin line of thought. It is possible, however, provided that we do not press the classification too far, roughly to classify technical pursuits according to the dominant science involved. We thus find a sixfold division, namely, (1) Geometrical techniques, (2) Mechanical techniques, (3) Physical techniques, (4) Chemical techniques, (5) Biological techniques, (6) Techniques of commerce and of social service.

By this division, it is meant that apart from auxiliary sciences some particular science requires emphasis in the training for most occupations. We can, for example, reckon carpentry, ironmongery, and many artistic crafts among geometrical techniques. Similarly agriculture is a biological technique. Probably cookery, if it includes food catering, would fall midway between biological, physical, and chemical sciences, though of this I am not sure.

The sciences associated with commerce and social service would be partly algebra, including arithmetic and statistics, and partly geography and history. But this section is somewhat heterogeneous in its scientific affinities. Anyhow the exact way in which technical pursuits are classified in relation to science is a detail. The essential point is, that with some thought it is possible to find scientific courses which illuminate most occupations. Furthermore, the problem is well understood, and has been brilliantly solved in many of the schools of technology and junior technical schools throughout the country.

In passing from science to literature, in our review of the intellectual elements of technical education, we note that many studies hover between the two: for example, history and geography. They are both of them very essential in education, provided that they are the right history and the right geography. Also books giving descriptive accounts of general results, and trains of thought in various sciences fall in the same category. Such books should be partly historical and partly expository of the main ideas which have finally arisen. Their value in education depends on their quality as mental stimulants. They must not be inflated with gas on the wonders of science, and must be informed with a broad outlook.

It is unfortunate that the literary element in education has rarely been considered apart from grammatical study. The historical reason is, that when the modern Platonic curriculum was being formed Latin and Greek were the sole keys which rendered great literature accessible. But there is no necessary connection between literature and grammar. The great age of Greek literature was already past before the arrival of the grammarians of Alexandria. Of all types of men to-day existing, classical scholars are the most remote from the Greeks of the Periclean times.

Mere literary knowledge is of slight importance. The only thing that matters is, how it is known. The facts related are nothing.

Literature only exists to express and develop that imaginative world which is our life, the kingdom which is within us. It follows that the literary side of a technical education should consist in an effort to make the pupils enjoy literature. It does not matter what they know, but the enjoyment is vital. The great English Universities, under whose direct authority school-children are examined in plays of Shakespeare, to the certain destruction of their enjoyment, should be prosecuted for soul murder.

Now there are two kinds of intellectual enjoyment: the enjoyment of creation, and the enjoyment of relaxation. They are not necessarily separated. A change of occupation may give the full tide of happiness which comes from the concurrence of both forms of pleasure. The appreciation of literature is really creation. The written word, its music, and its associations, are only the stimuli. The vision which they evoke is our own doing. No one, no genius other than our own, can make our own life live. But except for those engaged in literary occupations, literature is also a relaxation. It gives exercise to that other side which any occupation must suppress during the working hours. Art also has the same function in life as has literature.

To obtain the pleasure of relaxation requires no help. The pleasure is merely to cease doing. Some such pure relaxation is a necessary condition of health. Its dangers are notorious, and to the greater part of the necessary relaxation nature has affixed, not enjoyment, but the oblivion of sleep. Creative enjoyment is the outcome of successful effort and requires help for its initiation. Such enjoyment is necessary for high-speed work and for original achievement.

To speed up production with unrefreshed workmen is a disastrous economic policy. Temporary success will be at the expense of the nation, which, for long years of their lives, will have to support worn-out artisans-unemployables. Equally disastrous is the alternation of spasms of effort with periods of pure relaxation. Such periods are the seed-times of degeneration, unless rigorously curtailed. The normal recreation should be change of activity, satisfying the cravings of instincts. Games afford such activity. Their disconnection emphasises the relaxation, but their excess leaves us empty.

It is here that literature and art should play an essential part in a healthily organised nation. Their services to economic production would be only second to those of sleep or of food. I am not now talking of the training of an artist, but of the use of art as a condition of healthy life. It is analogous to sunshine in the physical world.

When we have once rid our minds of the idea that knowledge is to be exacted, there is no especial difficulty or expense involved in helping the growth of artistic enjoyment. All school-children could be sent at regular intervals to neighbouring theatres where suitable plays could be subsidised. Similarly for concerts and cinema films. Pictures are more doubtful in their popular attraction; but interesting representations of scenes or ideas which the children have read about would probably appeal. The pupils themselves should be encouraged in artistic efforts. Above all the art of reading aloud should be cultivated. The Roger de Coverley essays of Addison are perfect examples of readable prose.

Art and literature have not merely an indirect effect on the main energies of life. Directly, they give vision. The world spreads wide beyond the deliverances of material sense, with subtleties of reaction and with pulses of emotion. Vision is the necessary antecedent to control and to direction. In the contest of races which in its final issues will be decided in the workshops and not on the battlefield, the victory will belong to those who are masters of stores of trained nervous energy, working under conditions favourable to growth. One such essential condition is Art.

If there had been time, there are other things which I should like to have said: for example, to advocate the inclusion of one foreign language in all education. From direct observation I know this to be possible for artisan children. But enough has been put before you to make plain the principles with which we should undertake national education.

In conclusion, I recur to the thought of the Benedictines, who saved for mankind the vanishing civilisation of the ancient world by linking together knowledge, labour, and moral energy. Our danger is to conceive practical affairs as the kingdom of evil, in which success is only possible by the extrusion of ideal aims. I believe that such a conception is a fallacy directly negatived by practical experience. In education this error takes the form of a mean view of technical training. Our forefathers in the dark ages saved themselves by embodying high ideals in great organisations. It is our task, without servile imitation, boldly to exercise our creative energies.

CHAPTER V

The Place of Classics in Education

The future of classics in this country is not going mainly to be decided by the joy of classics to a finished scholar, and by the utility of scholarly training for scholarly avocations. The pleasure and the discipline of character to be derived from an education based mainly on classical literature and classical philosophy has been demonstrated by centuries of experience. The danger to classical learning does not arise because classical scholars now love classics less than their predecessors. It arises in this way. In the past classics reigned throughout the whole sphere of higher education. There were no rivals; and accordingly all students were steeped in classics throughout their school life, and its domination at the universities was only challenged by the narrow discipline of mathematics. There were many consequences to this state of things. There was a large demand for classical scholars for the mere purposes of tuition; there was a classical tone in all learned walks of life, so that aptitude for classics was a synonym for ability; and finally every boy who gave the slightest promise in that direction cultivated his natural or acquired interest in classical learning. All this is gone, and gone for ever. Humpty Dumpty was a good egg so long as he was on the top of the wall, but you can never set him up again. There are now other disciplines each involving topics of wide-spread interest, with complex relationships, and exhibiting in their development the noblest feats of genius in its stretch of imagination and its philosophic intuition. Almost every walk of life is now a learned profession, and demands one or more of these disciplines as the substratum for its

61

technical skill. Life is short, and the plastic period when the brain is apt for acquirement is still shorter. Accordingly, even if all children were fitted for it, it is absolutely impossible to maintain a system of education in which a complete training as a classical scholar is the necessary preliminary to the acquirement of other intellectual disciplines. As a member of the Prime Minister's Committee on the Place of Classics in Education it was my misfortune to listen to much ineffectual wailing from witnesses on the mercenary tendencies of modern parents. I do not believe that the modern parent of any class is more mercenary than his predecessors. When classics was the road to advancement, classics was the popular subject for study. Opportunity has now shifted its location, and classics is in danger. Was it not Aristotle who said that a good income was a desirable adjunct to an intellectual life? I wonder how Aristotle, as a parent, would have struck a headmaster of one of our great public schools. From my slight knowledge of Aristotle, I suspect that there would have been an argument, and that Aristotle would have got the best of it. I have been endeavouring to appreciate at its full value the danger which besets classics in the educational curriculum. The conclusion that I draw is that the future classics will be decided during the next few years in the secondary schools of this country. Within a generation the great public schools will have to follow suit, whether they like it or not.

The situation is dominated by the fact that in the future ninety per cent. of the pupils who leave school at the age of eighteen will never again read a classical book in the original. In the case of pupils leaving at an earlier age, the estimate of ninety per cent. may be changed to one of ninety-nine per cent. I have heard and read many a beautiful exposition of the value of classics to the scholar who reads Plato and Virgil in his armchair. But these people will never read classics either in their armchairs or in any other situation. We have got to produce a defence of classics which applies to this ninety per cent. of the pupils. If classics is swept out of the curriculum for this section, the remaining ten per cent. will soon vanish. No school will have the staff to teach them. The problem is urgent.

It would, however, be a great mistake to conclude that classics is faced with a hostile opinion either in the learned professions or from leaders of industry who have devoted attention to the relation between education and efficiency. The last discussion, public or private, on this subject, at which I have been present was a short and vigorous one at one of the leading committees of a great modern university. The three representatives of the Faculty of Science energetically urged the importance of classics on the ground of its value as a preliminary discipline for scientists. I mention this incident because in my experience it is typical.

We must remember that the whole problem of intellectual education is controlled by lack of time. If Methuselah was not a well-educated man, it was his own fault or that of his teachers. But our task is to deal with five years of secondary school-life. Classics can only be defended on the ground that within that period, and sharing that period with other subjects, it can produce a necessary enrichment of intellectual character more quickly than any alternative discipline directed to the same object.

In classics we endeavour by a thorough study of language to develop the mind in the regions of logic, philosophy, history and of æsthetic apprehension of literary beauty. The learning of the languages—Latin or Greek—is a subsidiary means for the furtherance of this ulterior object. When the object has been obtained, the languages can be dropped unless opportunity and choice lead to their further pursuit. There are certain minds, and among them some of the best, for which the analysis of language is not the avenue of approach to the goal of culture. For these a butterfly or a steam-engine has a wider range of significance than a Latin sentence. This is especially the case where there is a touch of genius arising from vivid apprehensions stimulating originality of thought. The assigned verbal sentence almost always says the wrong thing for such people, and confuses them by its trivial irrelevance.

But on the whole the normal avenue is the analysis of language. It represents the greatest common measure for the pupils, and by far the most manageable job for the teachers.

At this point I must cross-question myself. My other self asks me, Why do you not teach the children logic, if you want them to learn that subject? Wouldn't that be the obvious procedure? I answer in the words of a great man who to our infinite loss has recently died, Sanderson, the late headmaster of Oundle. His phrase was, They learn by contact. The meaning to be attached to this saying goes to the root of the true practice of education. It must start from the particular fact, concrete and definite for individual apprehension, and must gradually evolve towards the general idea. The devil to be avoided is the cramming of general statements which have no reference to individual personal experiences.

Now apply this principle to the determination of the best method to help a child towards a philosophical analysis of thought. I will put it in more homely style, What is the best way to make a child clear-headed in its thoughts and its statements? The general statements of a logic book have no reference to anything the child has ever heard of. They belong to the grown-up stage of education at— or not far from—the university. You must begin with the analysis of familiar English sentences. But this grammatical procedure, if prolonged beyond its elementary stages, is horribly dry. Furthermore, it has the disadvantage that it only analyses so far as the English language analyses. It does nothing to throw light upon the complex significance of English phrases, and words, and habits of mental procedure. Your next step is to teach the child a foreign language. Here you gain an enormous advantage. You get away from the nauseating formal drill for the drill's sake. The analysis is now automatic, while the pupil's attention is directed to expressing his wants in the language, or to understanding someone who is speaking to him, or to making out what an author has written. Every language embodies a definite type of mentality, and two languages necessarily display to the pupil some contrast between their two types. Common sense dictates that you start with French as early as possible in the child's life. If you are wealthy, you will provide a French nursery-governess. Less fortunate children will start French in a secondary school about the age of twelve. The direct method is probably used, by which the child is immersed in French throughout the lesson and is taught to think in French without the intervention of English between the French words and their significations. Even an average child will get on well, and soon acquires the power of handling and understanding simple French sentences. As I have said before, the gain is enormous; and, in addition, a useful instrument for after life is acquired. The sense for language grows, a sense which is the subconscious appreciation of language as an instrument of definite structure.

It is exactly now that the initiation of Latin is the best stimulus for mental expansion. The elements of Latin exhibit a peculiarly plain concrete case of language as a structure. Provided that your mind has grown to the level of that idea, the fact stares you in the face. You can miss it over English and French. Good English of a simple kind will go straight into slipshod French, and conversely good French will go into slipshod English. The difference between the slipshod French of the literal translation and the good French, which ought to have been written, is often rather subtle for that stage of mental growth, and is not always easy to explain. Both languages have the same common modernity of expression. But in the case of English and Latin the contrast of structure is obvious, and yet not so wide as to form an insuperable difficulty.

According to the testimony of schoolmasters, Latin is rather a popular subject; I know that as a schoolboy I enjoyed it myself. I believe that this popularity is due to the sense of enlightenment that accompanies its study. You know that you are finding out something. The words somehow stick in the sentences in a different way to what they do either in English or French, with odd queer differences of connotation. Of course in a way Latin is a more barbaric language than English. It is one step nearer to the sentence as the unanalysed unit.

This brings me to my next point. In my catalogue of the gifts of Latin I placed philosophy between logic and history. In this connection, that is its true place. The philosophic instinct which Latin evokes, hovers between the two and enriches both. The analysis of thought involved in translation, English to Latin or Latin to English, imposes that type of experience which is the necessary introduction to philosophic logic. If in after life your job is to think, render thanks to Providence which ordained that, for five years of your youth, you did a Latin prose once a week and daily construed some Latin author. The introduction to any subject is the process of learning by contact. To that majority of people for whom language is the readiest stimulus to thought-activity, the road towards enlightenment of understanding runs from simple English grammar to French, from French to Latin, and also traverses the elements of Geometry and of Algebra. I need not remind my readers that I can claim Plato's authority for the general principle which I am upholding.

From the philosophy of thought we now pass to the philosophy of history. I again recur to Sanderson's great saying, They learn by contact. How on earth is a child to learn history by contact? The original documents, charters and laws and diplomatic correspondence, are double Dutch to it. A game of football is perhaps a faint reflection of the Battle of Marathon. But that is only to say that human life in all ages and circumstances has common qualities. Furthermore, all this diplomatic and political stuff with which we cram children is a very thin view of history. What is really necessary is that we should have an instinctive grasp of the flux of outlook, and of thought, and of æsthetic and racial impulses, which have controlled the troubled history of mankind. Now the Roman Empire is the bottleneck through which the vintage of the past has passed into modern life. So far as European civilisation is concerned the key to history is a comprehension of the mentality of Rome and the work of its Empire.

In the language of Rome, embodying in literary form the outlook of Rome, we possess the simplest material, by contact with which we can gain appreciation of the tides of change in human affairs. The mere obvious relations of the languages, French and English, to Latin are in themselves a philosophy of history. Consider the contrast which English presents to French: the entire break of English with the civilised past of Britain and the slow creeping back of words and phrases of Mediterranean origin with their cargoes of civilised meaning: in French we have continuity of development, amid obvious traces of rude shock. I am not asking for pretentious abstract lectures on such points. The thing illustrates itself. An elementary knowledge of French and Latin with a mother-tongue of English imparts the requisite atmosphere of reality to the story of the racial wanderings which created our Europe. Language is the incarnation of the mentality of the race which fashioned it. Every phrase and word embodies some habitual idea of men and women as they ploughed their fields, tended their homes, and built their cities. For this reason there are no true synonyms as between words and phrases in different languages. The whole of what I have been saying is merely an embroidery upon this single theme, and our endeavour to emphasise its critical importance. In English, French, and Latin we possess a triangle, such that one pair of vertices, English and French, exhibits a pair of diverse expressions of two chief types of modern mentality, and the relations of these vertices to the third exhibit alternative processes of derivation from the Mediterranean civilisation of the past. This is the essential triangle of literary culture, containing within itself freshness of contrast, embracing both the present and the past. It ranges through space and time. These are the grounds by which we justify the assertion, that in the acquirement of French and Latin is to be found the easiest mode of learning by contact the philosophy of logic and the philosophy of history. Apart from some such intimate experience, your analyses of thought and your histories of actions are mere sounding brasses. I am not claiming, and I do not for a moment believe, that this route of education is more than the simplest, easiest route for the majority of pupils. I am certain that there is a large minority for which the emphasis should be different. But I do believe that it is the route which can give the greatest success for the largest majority. It has also the advantage of having survived the test of experience. I believe that large modifications require to be introduced into existing practice to adapt it for present needs. But on the whole this foundation of literary education involves the best understood tradition and the largest corps of experienced scholarly teachers who can realise it in practice.

The reader has perhaps observed that I have as yet said nothing of the glories of Roman literature. Of course the teaching of Latin must proceed by the means of reading Latin literature with the pupils. This literature possesses vigorous authors who have succeeded in putting across the footlights the Roman mentality on a variety of topics, including its appreciation of Greek thought. One of the merits of Roman literature is its comparative lack of outstanding genius. There is very little aloofness about its authors, they express their race and very little which is beyond all differences of race. With the exception of Lucretius, you always feel the limitations under which they are working. Tacitus expressed the views of the Die-hards of the Roman Senate, and, blind to the achievements of Roman provincial administration, could only see that Greek freedmen were replacing Roman aristocrats. The Roman Empire and the mentality which created it absorbed the genius of Romans. Very little of Roman literature will find its way into the kingdom of heaven, when the events of this world will have lost their importance. The languages of heaven will be Chinese, Greek, French, German, Italian, and English, and the blessed Saints will dwell with delight on these golden expressions of eternal life. They will be wearied with the moral fervour of Hebrew literature in its battle with a vanished evil, and with Roman authors who have mistaken the Forum for the footstool of the living God.

We do not teach Latin in the hope that Roman authors, read in the original, may be for our pupils companions through life. English literature is so much greater: it is richer, deeper, and more subtle. If your tastes are philosophic, would you abandon Bacon and Hobbes, Locke, Berkeley, Hume, and Mill for the sake of Cicero? Not unless your taste among the moderns would lead you to Martin Tupper. Perhaps you crave for reflection on the infinite variety of human existence and the reaction of character to circumstance. Would you exchange Shakespeare and the English novelists for Terence, Plautus, and the banquet of Trimalchio? Then there are our humorists, Sheridan, Dickens, and others. Did anyone ever laugh like that as he read a Latin author? Cicero was a great orator, staged amid the pomp of Empire. England also can show statesmen inspired to expound policies with imagination. I will not weary you with an extended catalogue embracing poetry and history. I simply wish to justify my scepticism as to the claim for Latin literature that it expresses with outstanding perfection the universal element in human life. It cannot laugh and it can hardly cry.

You must not tear it from its context. It is not a literature in the sense that Greece and England have produced literatures, expressions of universal human feeling. Latin has one theme and that is Rome—Rome, the mother of Europe, and the great Babylon, the harlot whose doom is described by the writer of the Apocalypse:

"Standing afar off for the fear of her torment, saying, Alas, alas, that great city Babylon, that mighty city! for in one hour is thy judgment come. And the merchants of the earth shall weep and mourn over her; for no man buyeth their merchandise any more:

"The merchandise of gold, and silver, and precious stones, and of pearls, and fine linen, and purple, and silk, and scarlet, and all thyine wood, and all manner vessels of ivory, and all manner vessels of most precious wood, and of brass, and iron, and marble;

"And cinnamon, and odours, and ointments, and frankincense, and wine, and oil, and fine flour, and wheat, and beasts, and sheep, and horses, and chariots, and slaves, and souls of men."

This is the way Roman civilisation appeared to an early Christian. But then Christianity itself is part of the outcrop of the ancient world which Rome passed on to Europe. We inherit the dual aspect of the civilisations of the eastern Mediterranean.

The function of Latin literature is its expression of Rome. When to England and France your imagination can add Rome in the background, you have laid firm the foundations of culture. The understanding of Rome leads back to that Mediterranean civilisation of which Rome was the last phase, and it automatically exhibits the geography of Europe, and the functions of seas and rivers and mountains and plains. The merit of this study in the education of youth is its concreteness, its inspiration to action, and the uniform greatness of persons, in their characters and their staging. Their aims were great, their virtues were great, and their vices were great. They had the saving merit of sinning with cart-ropes. Moral education is impossible apart from the habitual vision of greatness. If we are not great, it does not matter what we do or what is the issue. Now the sense of greatness is an immediate intuition and not the conclusion of an argument. It is permissible for youth in the agonies of religious conversion to entertain the feeling of being a worm and no man, so long as there remains the conviction of greatness sufficient to justify the eternal wrath of God. The sense of greatness is the groundwork of morals. We are at the threshold of a democratic age, and it remains to be determined whether the equality of man is to be realised on a high level or a low level. There was never a time in which it was more essential to hold before the young the vision of Rome: in itself a great drama, and with issues greater than itself. We are now already immersed in the topic of æsthetic appreciation of literary quality. It is here that the tradition of classical teaching requires most vigorous reformation for adaptation to new conditions. It is obsessed with the formation of finished classical scholars. The old tradition was remorselessly to devote the initial stages to the acquirement of the languages and then to trust to the current literary atmosphere to secure enjoyment of the literature. During the latter part of the nineteenth century other subjects encroached on the available time. Too often the result has been merely time wasted in the failure to learn the language. I often think that the ruck of pupils from great English schools show a deplorable lack of intellectual zest, arising from this sense of failure. The school course of classics must be planned so that a definite result is clearly achieved. There has been too great a product of failures on the road to an ambitious ideal of scholarship.

In approaching every work of art we have to comport ourselves suitably in regard to two factors, scale and pace. It is not fair to the architect if you examine St. Peter's at Rome with a microscope, and the Odyssey becomes insipid if you read it at the rate of five lines a day. Now the problem before us is exactly this. We are dealing with pupils who will never know Latin well enough to read it quickly, and the vision to be illumed is of vast scale, set in the history of all time. A careful study of scale and pace, and of the correlative functions of various parts of our work, should appear to be essential. I have not succeeded in hitting upon any literature which deals with this question with reference to the psychology of the pupils. Is it a masonic secret?

I have often noticed that, if in an assembly of great scholars the topic of translations be introduced, they function as to their emotions and sentiments in exactly the same way as do decent people in the presence of a nasty sex-problem. A mathematician has no scholastic respectability to lose, so I will face the question.

It follows from the whole line of thought which I have been developing, that an exact appreciation of the meanings of Latin words, of the ways in which ideas are connected in grammatical constructions, and of the whole hang of a Latin sentence with its distribution of emphasis, forms the very backbone of the merits which I ascribe to the study of Latin. Accordingly any woolly vagueness of teaching, slurring over the niceties of language defeats the whole ideal which I have set before you. The use of a translation to enable the pupils to get away from the Latin as quickly as possible, or to avoid the stretch of mind in grappling with construction, is erroneous. Exactness, definiteness, and independent power of analysis are among the main prizes of the whole study.

But we are still confronted with the inexorable problem of pace, and with the short four or five years of the whole course. Every poem is meant to be read within certain limits of time. The contrasts, and the images, and the transition of moods must correspond with the sway of rhythms in the human spirit. These have their periods, which refuse to be stretched beyond certain limits. You may take the noblest poetry in the world, and, if you stumble through it at snail's pace, it collapses from a work of art into a rubbish heap. Think of the child's mind as he pores over his work: he reads "as when," then follows a pause with a reference to the dictionary, then he goes on—"an eagle," then another reference to the dictionary, followed by a period of wonderment over the construction, and so on, and so on. Is that going to help him to the vision of Rome? Surely, surely, common sense dictates that you procure the best literary translation you can, the one which best preserves the charm and vigour of the original, and that you read it aloud at the right pace, and append such comments as will elucidate the comprehension. The attack on the Latin will then be fortified by the sense that it enshrines a living work of art.

But someone objects that a translation is woefully inferior to the original. Of course it is, that is why the boy has to master the Latin original. When the original has been mastered, it can be given its proper pace. I plead for an initial sense of the unity of the whole, to be given by a translation at the right pace, and for a final appreciation of the full value of the whole to be given by the original at the right pace. Wordsworth talks of men of science who "murder to dissect." In the past, classical scholars have been veritable assassins compared to them. The sense of beauty is eager and vehement, and should be treated with the reverence which is its due. But I go further. The total bulk of Latin literature necessary to convey the vision of Rome is much greater than the students can possibly accomplish in the original. They should read more Virgil than they can read in Latin, more Lucretius than they can read in Latin, more history than they can read in Latin, more Cicero than they can read in Latin. In the study of an author the selected portions in Latin should illumine a fuller disclosure of his whole mind, although without the force of his own words in his own language. It is, however, a grave evil if no part of an author be read in his own original words.

The difficulty of scale is largely concerned in the presentation of classical history. Everything set before the young must be rooted in the particular and the individual. Yet we want to illustrate the general characters of whole periods. We must make students learn by contact. We can exhibit the modes of life by visual representations. There are photographs of buildings, casts of statues, and pictures from vases or frescoes illustrating religious myths or domestic scenes. In this way we can compare Rome with the preceding civilisation of the eastern Mediterranean, and with the succeeding period of the Middle Ages. It is essential to get into the children's minds how men altered, in their appearance, their dwellings, their technology, their art, and their religious beliefs. We must imitate the procedure of the zoologists who have the whole of animal creation on their hands. They teach by demonstrating typical examples. We must do likewise, to exhibit the position of Rome in history.

The life of man is founded on Technology, Science, Art and Religion. All four are inter-connected and issue from his total mentality. But there are particular intimacies between Science and Technology, and between Art and Religion. No social organisation can be understood without reference to these four underlying factors. A modern steam-engine does the work of a thousand slaves in the ancient world. Slave-raiding was the key to much of the ancient imperialism. A modern printing-press is an essential adjunct to a modern democracy. The key to modern mentality is the continued advance of science with the consequential shift of ideas and progress of technology. In the ancient world Mesopotamia and Egypt were made possible by irrigation. But the Roman Empire existed by virtue of the grandest application of technology that the world had hitherto seen: its roads, its bridges, its aqueducts, its tunnels, its sewers, its vast buildings, its organised merchant navies, its military science, its metallurgy, and its agriculture. This was the secret of the extension and the unity of Roman civilisation. I have often wondered why Roman engineers did not invent the steam-engine. They might have done it at any time, and then how different would have been the history of the world. I ascribe it to the fact that they lived in a warm climate and had not introduced tea and coffee. In the eighteenth century thousands of men sat by fires and watched their kettles boil. We all know of course that Hiero of Alexandria invented some slight anticipation. All that was wanted was that the Roman engineers should have been impressed with the motive force of steam by the humble process of watching their kettles.

The history of mankind has yet to be set in its proper relation to the gathering momentum of technological advance. Within the last hundred years, a developed science has wedded itself to a developed technology and a new epoch has opened.

Similarly about a thousand years before Christ the first great literary epoch commenced when the art of writing was finally popularised. In its earlier dim origins the art had been used for traditional hieratic formulæ and for the formal purposes of governmental record and chronicle. It is a great mistake to think that in the past the full sweep of a new invention has ever been anticipated at its first introduction. It is not even so at the present day, when we are all trained to meditate on the possibilities of new ideas. But in the past, with its different direction of thought, novelty slowly ate its way into the social system. Accordingly writing, as a stimulus to the preservation of individual novelty of thought, was but slowly grasped on the borders of the eastern Mediterranean. When the realisation of its possibilities was complete, in the hands of the Greeks and the Hebrews, civilisation took a new turn; though the general influence of Hebrew mentality was delayed for a thousand years till the advent of Christianity. But it was now that their prophets were recording their inward thoughts, when Greek civilisation was beginning to take shape.

What I want to illustrate is that in the large scale treatment of history necessary for the background and the foreground of the vision of Rome, the consecutive chronicle of political events on the scale traditional to our histories absolutely vanishes. Even verbal explanations partly go into the background. We must utilise models, and pictures, and diagrams, and charts to exhibit typical examples of the growth of technology and its impact on the current modes of life. In the same way art, in its curious fusion with utility and with religion, both expresses the actual inward life of imagination and changes it by its very expression. The children can see the art of previous epochs in models and pictures, and sometimes the very objects in museums. The treatment of the history of the past must not start with generalised statements, but with concrete examples exhibiting the slow succession of period to period, and of mode of life to mode of life, and of race to race.

The same concreteness of treatment must apply when we come to the literary civilisations of the eastern Mediterranean. When you come to think of it, the whole claim for the importance of classics rests on the basis that there is no substitute for first-hand knowledge. In so far as Greece and Rome are the founders of European civilisation, a knowledge of history means above all things a first-hand knowledge of the thoughts of Greeks and Romans. Accordingly, to put the vision of Rome into its proper setting, I urge that the pupils should read at first hand some few examples of Greek literature. Of course it must be in translation. But I prefer a translation of what a Greek actually said, to any talk about the Greeks written by an Englishman, however well he has done it. Books about Greece should come after some direct knowledge of Greece.

The sort of reading I mean is a verse translation of the Odyssey, some Herodotus, some choruses of plays translated by Gilbert Murray, some lives of Plutarch, especially the part about Archimedes in the life of Marcellus, and the definitions and axioms and one or two propositions from Euclid's Elements in the exact scholarly translation of Heath. In all this, just enough explanation is wanted to give the mental environment of the authors. The marvellous position of Rome in relation to Europe comes from the fact that it has transmitted to us a double inheritance. It received the Hebrew religious thought, and has passed on to Europe its fusion with Greek civilisation. Rome itself stands for the impress of organization and unity upon diverse fermenting elements. Roman Law embodies the secret of Roman greatness in its Stoic respect for intimate rights of human nature within an iron framework of empire. Europe is always flying apart because of the diverse explosive character of its inheritance, and coming together because it can never shake off that impress of unity it has received from Rome. The history of Europe is the history of Rome curbing the Hebrew and the Greek, with their various impulses of religion, and of science, and of art, and of quest for material comfort, and of lust of domination, which are all at daggers drawn with each other. The vision of Rome is the vision of the unity of civilisation.

CHAPTER VI

The Mathematical Curriculum

The situation in regard to education at the present time cannot find its parallel without going back for some centuries to the break-up of the mediæval traditions of learning. Then, as now, the traditional intellectual outlook, despite the authority which it had justly acquired from its notable triumphs, had grown to be too narrow for the interests of mankind. The result of this shifting of human interest was a demand for a parallel shifting of the basis of education, so as to fit the pupils for the ideas which later in life would in fact occupy their minds. Any serious fundamental change in the intellectual outlook of human society must necessarily be followed by an educational revolution. It may be delayed for a generation by vested interests or by the passionate attachment of some leaders of thought to the cycle of ideas within which they received their own mental stimulus at an impressionable age. But the law is inexorable that education to be living and effective must be directed to informing pupils with those ideas, and to creating for them those capacities which will enable them to appreciate the current thought of their epoch.

There is no such thing as a successful system of education in a vacuum, that is to say, a system which is divorced from immediate contact with the existing intellectual atmosphere. Education which is not modern shares the fate of all organic things which are kept too long.

But the blessed word "modern" does not really solve our difficulties. What we mean is, relevant to modern thought, either in the ideas imparted or in the aptitudes produced. Something found out only yesterday may not really be modern in this sense. It may belong to some bygone system of thought prevalent in a previous age, or, what is very much more likely, it may be too recondite. When we demand that education should be relevant to modern thought, we are referring to thoughts broadly spread throughout cultivated society. It is this question of the unfitness of recondite subjects for use in general education which I wish to make the keynote of my address this afternoon.

It is in fact rather a delicate subject for mathematicians. Outsiders are apt to accuse our subject of being recondite. Let us grasp the nettle at once and frankly admit that in general opinion it is the very typical example of reconditeness. By this word I do not mean difficulty, but that the ideas involved are of highly special application, and rarely influence thought.

This liability to reconditeness is the characteristic evil which is apt to destroy the utility of mathematics in liberal education. So far as it clings to the educational use of the subject, so far we must acquiesce in a miserably low level of mathematical attainment among cultivated people in general. I yield to no one in my anxiety to increase the educational scope of mathematics. The way to achieve this end is not by a mere blind demand for more mathematics. We must face the real difficulty which obstructs its extended use.

Is the subject recondite? Now, viewed as a whole, I think it is. *Securus judicat orbis terrarum*—the general judgment of mankind is sure.

The subject as it exists in the minds and in the books of students of mathematics *is* recondite. It proceeds by deducing innumerable special results from general ideas, each result more recondite than the preceding. It is not my task this afternoon to defend mathematics as a subject for profound study. It can very well take care of itself. What I want to emphasise is, that the very reasons which make this science a delight to its students are reasons which obstruct its use as an educational instrument—namely, the boundless wealth of deductions from the interplay of general theorems, their complication, their apparent remoteness from the ideas from which the argument started, the variety of methods, and their purely abstract character which brings, as its gift, eternal truth.

Of course, all these characteristics are of priceless value to students; for ages they have fascinated some of the keenest intellects. My only remark is that, except for a highly selected class, they are fatal in education. The pupils are bewildered by a multiplicity of detail, without apparent relevance either to great ideas or to ordinary thoughts. The extension of this sort of training in the direction of acquiring more detail is the last measure to be desired in the interests of education.

The conclusion at which we arrive is, that mathematics, if it is to be used in general education, must be subjected to a rigorous process of selection and adaptation. I do not mean, what is of course obvious, that however much time we devote to the subject the average pupil will not get very far. But that, however limited the progress, certain characteristics of the subject, natural at any stage, must be rigorously excluded. The science as presented to young pupils must lose its aspect of reconditeness. It must, on the face of it, deal directly and simply with a few general ideas of far-reaching importance.

Now, in this matter of the reform of mathematical instruction, the present generation of teachers may take a very legitimate pride in its achievements. It has shown immense energy in reform, and has accomplished more than would have been thought possible in so short a time. It is not always recognised how difficult is the task of changing a well-established curriculum entrenched behind public examinations.

But for all that, great progress has been made, and, to put the matter at its lowest, the old dead tradition has been broken up. I want to indicate this afternoon the guiding idea which should direct our efforts at reconstruction. I have already summed it up in a phrase, namely, we must aim at the elimination of reconditeness from the educational use of the subject.

Our courses of instruction should be planned to illustrate simply a succession of ideas of obvious importance. All pretty divagations should be rigorously excluded. The goal to be aimed at is that the pupil should acquire familiarity with abstract thought, should realise how it applies to particular concrete circumstances, and should know how to apply general methods to its logical investigation. With this educational ideal nothing can be worse than the aimless accretion of theorems in our text-books, which acquire their position merely because the children can be made to learn them and examiners can set neat questions on them. The bookwork to be learnt should all be very important as illustrating ideas. The examples set—and let there be as many examples as teachers find necessary—should be direct illustrations of the theorems, either by way of abstract particular cases or by way of application to concrete phenomena. Here it is worth remarking that it is quite useless to simplify the bookwork, if the examples set in examinations in fact require an extended knowledge of recondite details. There is a mistaken idea that problems test ability and genius, and that bookwork tests cram. This is not my experience. Only boys who have been specially crammed for scholarships can ever do a problem paper successfully. Bookwork properly set, not in mere snippets according to the usual bad plan, is a far better test of ability, provided that it is supplemented by direct examples. But this is a digression on the bad influence of examinations on teaching.

The main ideas which lie at the base of mathematics are not at all recondite. They are abstract. But one of the main objects of the inclusion of mathematics in a liberal education is to train the pupils to handle abstract ideas. The science constitutes the first large group of abstract ideas which naturally occur to the mind in any precise form. For the purposes of education, mathematics consists of the relations of number, the relations of quantity, and the relations of space. This is not a general definition of mathematics, which, in my opinion, is a much more general science. But we are now discussing the use of mathematics in education. These three groups of relations, concerning number, quantity, and space, are interconnected.

Now, in education we proceed from the particular to the general. Accordingly, children should be taught the use of these ideas by practice among simple examples. My point is this: The goal should be, not an aimless accumulation of special mathematical theorems, but the final recognition that the preceding years of work have illustrated those relations of number, and of quantity, and of space, which are of fundamental importance. Such a training should lie at the base of all philosophical thought. In fact elementary mathematics rightly conceived would give just that philosophical discipline of which the ordinary mind is capable. But what at all costs we ought to avoid, is the pointless accumulation of details. As many examples as you like; let the children work at them for terms, or for years. But these examples should be direct illustrations of the main ideas. In this way, and this only, can the fatal reconditeness be avoided.

I am not now speaking in particular of those who are to be professional mathematicians, o or of those who for professional reasons require a knowledge of certain mathematical details. We are considering the liberal education of all students, including these two classes. This general use of mathematics should be the simple study of a few general truths, well illustrated by practical examples. This study should be conceived by itself, and completely separated in idea from the professional study mentioned above, for which it would make a most excellent preparation. Its final stage should be the recognition of the general truths which the work done has illustrated. As far as I can make out, at present the final stage is the proof of some property of circles connected with triangles. Such properties are immensely interesting to mathematicians. But are they not rather recondite, and what is the precise relation of such theorems to the ideal of a liberal education? The end of all the grammatical studies of the student in classics is to read Virgil and Horace—the greatest thoughts of the greatest men. Are we content, when pleading for the adequate representation in education of our own science, to say that the end of a mathematical training is that the student should know the properties of the nine-point circle? I ask you frankly, is it not rather a "come down"?

This generation of mathematical teachers has done so much strenuous work in the way of reorganising mathematical instruction that there is no need to despair of its being able to elaborate a curriculum which shall leave in the minds of the pupils something even nobler than "the ambiguous case."

Let us think how this final review, closing the elementary course, might be conducted for the more intelligent pupils. Partly no doubt it requires a general oversight of the whole work done, considered without undue detail so as to emphasise the general ideas used, and their possibilities of importance when subjected to further study. Also the analytical and geometrical ideas find immediate application in the physical laboratory where a course of simple experimental mechanics should have been worked through. Here the point of view is twofold, the physical ideas and the mathematical ideas illustrate each other.

The mathematical ideas are essential to the precise formulation of the mechanical laws. The idea of a precise law of nature, the extent to which such laws are in fact verified in our experience, and the role of abstract thought in their formulation, then become practically apparent to the pupil. The whole topic of course requires detailed development with full particular illustration, and is not suggested as requiring merely a few bare abstract statements.

It would, however, be a grave error to put too much emphasis on the mere process of direct explanation of the previous work by way of final review. My point is, that the latter end of the course should be so selected that in fact the general ideas underlying all the previous mathematical work should be brought into prominence. This may well be done by apparently entering on a new subject. For example, the ideas of quantity and the ideas of number are fundamental to all precise thought. In the previous stages they will not have been sharply separated; and children are, rightly enough, pushed on to algebra without too much bother and quantity. But the more intelligent among them at the end of their curriculum would gain immensely by a careful consideration of those fundamental properties of quantity in general which lead to the introduction of numerical measurement. This is a topic which also has the advantage that the necessary books are actually to hand. Euclid's fifth book is regarded by those qualified to judge as one of the triumphs of Greek mathematics. It deals with this very point. Nothing can be more characteristic of the hopelessly illiberal character of the traditional mathematical education than the fact that this book has always been omitted. It deals with ideas, and therefore was ostracised. Of course a careful selection of the more important propositions and a careful revision of the argument are required. The whole book would not be wanted, but just the few propositions which embody the fundamental ideas. The subject is not fit for backward pupils; but certainly it could be made interesting to the more advanced class. There would be great scope for interesting discussion as to the nature of quantity, and the tests which we should apply to ascertain when we are dealing with quantities. The work would not be at all in the air, but would be illustrated at every stage by reference to actual examples of cases where the quantitative character is absent, or obscure, or doubtful, or evident. Temperature, heat, electricity, pleasure and pain, mass and distance could all be considered.

Another idea which requires illustration is that of functionality. A function in analysis is the counterpart of a law in the physical universe, and of a curve in geometry. Children have studied the relations of functions to curves from the first beginning of their study of algebra, namely in drawing graphs. Of recent years there has been a great reform in respect to graphs. But at its present stage it has either gone too far or not far enough. It is not enough merely to draw a graph. The idea behind the graph—like the man behind the gun—is essential in order to make it effective. At present there is some tendency merely to set the children to draw curves, and there to leave the whole question.

In the study of simple algebraic functions and of trigonometrical functions we are initiating the study of the precise expression of physical laws. Curves are another way of representing these laws. The simple fundamental laws—such as the inverse square and the direct distance—should be passed under review, and the applications of the simple functions to express important concrete cases of physical laws considered. I cannot help thinking that the final review of this topic might well take the form of a study of some of the main ideas of the differential calculus applied to simple curves. There is nothing particularly difficult about the conception of a rate of change; and the differentiation of a few powers of x, such as x^2, x^3, etc., could easily be effected; perhaps by the aid of geometry even $\sin x$ and $\cos x$ could be differentiated. If we once abandon our fatal habit of cramming the children with theorems which they do not understand, and will never use, there will be plenty of time to concentrate their attention on really important topics. We can give them familiarity with conceptions which really influence thought.

Before leaving this topic of physical laws and mathematical functions, there are other points to be noticed. The fact that the precise law is never really verified by observation in its full precision is capable of easy illustration and of affording excellent examples. Again, statistical laws, namely laws which are only satisfied on the average by large numbers, can easily be studied and illustrated. In fact a slight study of statistical methods and their application to social phenomena affords one of the simplest examples of the application of algebraic ideas.

Another way in which the students' ideas can be generalised is by the use of the History of Mathematics, conceived not as a mere assemblage of the dates and names of men, but as an exposition of the general current of thought which occasioned the subjects to be objects of interest at the time of their first elaboration. I merely draw attention to it now, to point out that perhaps it is the very subject which may best obtain the results for which I am pleading.

We have indicated two main topics, namely general ideas of quantity and of laws of nature, which should be an object of study in the mathematical curriculum of a liberal education. But there is another side to mathematics which must not be overlooked. It is the chief instrument for discipline in logical method.

Now, what is logical method, and how can any one be trained in it?

Logical method is more than the mere knowledge of valid types of reasoning and practice in the concentration of mind necessary to follow them. If it were only this, it would still be very important; for the human mind was not evolved in the bygone ages for the sake of reasoning, but merely to enable mankind with more art to hunt between meals for fresh food supplies. Accordingly few people can follow close reasoning without considerable practice.

More than this is wanted to make a good reasoner, or even to enlighten ordinary people with knowledge of what constitutes the essence of the art. The art of reasoning consists in getting hold of the subject at the right end, of seizing on the few general ideas which illuminate the whole, and of persistently marshalling all subsidiary facts round them. Nobody can be a good reasoner unless by constant practice he has realised the importance of getting hold of the big ideas and of hanging on to them like grim death. For this sort of training geometry is, I think, better than algebra. The field of thought of algebra is rather obscure, whereas space is an obvious insistent thing evident to all. Then the process of simplification, or abstraction, by which all irrelevant properties of matter, such as colour, taste, and weight, are put aside is an education in itself. Again, the definitions, and the propositions assumed without proof, illustrate the necessity of forming clear notions of the fundamental facts of the subject-matter and of the relations between them. All this belongs to the mere prolegomena of the subject. When we come to its development, its excellence increases. The learner is not initially confronted with any symbolism which bothers the memory by its rules, however simple they may be. Also, from the very beginning the reasoning, if properly conducted, is dominated by well-marked ideas which guide each stage of development. Accordingly the essence of logical method receives immediate exemplification.

Let us now put aside for the moment the limitations introduced by the dullness of average pupils and the pressure on time due to other subjects, and consider what geometry has to offer in the way of a liberal education. I will indicate some stages in the subject, without meaning that necessarily they are to be studied in this exclusive order. The first stage is the study of *congruence*. Our perception of congruence is in practice dependent on our judgments of the invariability of the intrinsic properties of bodies when their external circumstances are varying. But however it arises, congruence is in essence the correlation of two regions of space, point by point, so that all homologous distances and all homologous angles are equal. It is to be noticed that the definition of the equality of lengths and angles is their congruence, and all tests of equality, such as the use of the yard measure, are merely devices for making immediate judgments of congruence easy. I make these remarks to suggest that apart from the reasoning connected with it, congruence, both as an example of a larger and very far-reaching idea and also for its own sake, is well worthy of attentive consideration. The propositions concerning it elucidate the elementary properties of the triangle, the parallelogram, and the circle, and of the relations of two planes to each other. It is very desirable to restrict the proved propositions of this part within the narrowest bounds, partly by assuming redundant axiomatic propositions, and partly by introducing only those propositions of absolutely fundamental importance.

The second stage is the study of similarity. This can be reduced to three or four fundamental propositions. Similarity is an enlargement of the idea of congruence, and, like that idea, is another example of a one-to-one correlation of points of spaces. Any extension of study of this subject might well be in the direction of the investigation of one or two simple properties of similar and similarly situated rectilinear figures. The whole subject receives its immediate applications in plans and maps. It is important, however, to remember that trigonometry is really the method by which the main theorems are made available for use.

The third stage is the study of the elements of trigonometry. This is the study of the periodicity introduced by rotation and of properties preserved in a correlation of similar figures. Here for the first time we introduce a slight use of the algebraic analysis founded on the study of number and quantity. The importance of the periodic character of the functions requires full illustration. The simplest properties of the functions are the only ones required for the solution of triangles, and the consequent applications to surveying. The wealth of formulæ, often important in themselves, but entirely useless for this type of study, which crowd our books should be rigorously excluded, except so far as they are capable of being proved by the pupils as direct examples of the bookwork.

This question of the exclusion of formulæ is best illustrated by considering this example of Trigonometry, though of course I may well have hit on an unfortunate case in which my judgment is at fault. A great part of the educational advantage of the subject can be obtained by confining study to Trigonometry of one angle and by exclusion of the addition formulæ for the sine and cosine and the sum of two angles. The functions can be graphed, and the solution of triangles effected. Thus the aspects of the science as (1) embodying analytically the immediate results of some of the theorems deduced from congruence and similarity, (2) as a solution of the main problem of surveying, (3) as a study of the fundamental functions required to express periodicity and wave motion, will all be impressed on the pupils' minds both by bookwork and example.

If it be desired to extend this course, the addition formulæ should be added. But great care should be taken to exclude specialising the pupils in the wealth of formulæ which comes in their train. By "exclude" is meant that the pupils should not have spent time or energy in acquiring any facility in their deduction. The teacher may find it interesting to work a few such examples before a class. But such results are not among those which learners need retain. Also, I would exclude the whole subject of circumscribed and inscribed circles both from Trigonometry and from the previous geometrical courses. It is all very pretty, but I do not understand what its function is in an elementary non-professional curriculum.

Accordingly, the actual bookwork of the subject is reduced to very manageable proportions. I was told the other day of an American college where the students are expected to know by heart ninety formulæ or results in Trigonometry alone. We are not quite so bad as that. In fact, in Trigonometry we have nearly approached the ideal here sketched out as far as our elementary courses are concerned.

The fourth stage introduces Analytical Geometry. The study of graphs in algebra has already employed the fundamental notions, and all that is now required is a rigorously pruned course on the straight line, the circle, and the three types of conic sections, defined by the forms of their equations. At this point there are two remarks to be made. It is often desirable to give our pupils mathematical information which we do not prove. For example, in co-ordinate geometry, the reduction of the general equation of the second degree is probably beyond the capacities of most of the type of students whom we are considering. But that need not prevent us from explaining the fundamental position of conics, as exhausting the possible types of such curves.

The second remark is to advocate the entire sweeping away of 'geometrical conics' as a separate subject. Naturally, on suitable occasions the analysis of analytical geometry will be lightened by the use of direct deduction from some simple figure. But geometrical conics, as developed from the definition of a conic section by the focus and directrix property, suffers from glaring defects. It is hopelessly recondite. The fundamental definition of a conic, $SP = e \cdot PM$, usual in this subject at this stage, is thoroughly bad. It is very recondite, and has no obvious importance. Why should such curves be studied at all, any more than those defined by an indefinite number of other formulæ? But when we have commenced the study of the Cartesian methods, the equations of the first and second degrees are naturally the first things to think about.

In this ideal course of Geometry, the fifth stage is occupied with the elements of Projective Geometry. The general ideas of cross ratio and of projection are here fundamental. Projection is yet a more general instance of that one-to-one correlation which we have already considered under congruence and similarity. Here again we must avoid the danger of being led into a bewildering wealth of detail.

The intellectual idea which projective geometry is to illustrate is the importance in reasoning of the correlation of all cases which can be proved to possess in common certain identical properties. The preservation of the projective properties in projection is the one important educational idea of the subject. Cross ratio only enters as the fundamental metrical property which is preserved. The few propositions considered are selected to illustrate the two allied processes which are made possible by this procedure. One is proof by simplification. Here the simplification is psychological and not logical—for the general case is logically the simplest. What is meant is: Proof by considering the case which is in fact the most familiar to us, or the easiest to think about. The other procedure is the deduction of particular cases from known general truths, as soon as we have a means of discovering such cases or a criterion for testing them.

The projective definition of conic sections and the identity of the results obtained with the curves derived from the general equation of the second degree are capable of simple exposition, but lie on the border-line of the subject. It is the sort of topic on which information can be given, and the proofs suppressed.

The course of geometry as here conceived in its complete ideal—and ideals can never be realised—is not a long one. The actual amount of mathematical deduction at each stage in the form of bookwork is very slight. But much more explanation would be given, the importance of each proposition being illustrated by examples, either worked out or for students to work, so selected as to indicate the fields of thought to which it applies. By such a course the student would gain an analysis of the leading properties of space, and of the chief methods by which they are investigated.

The study of the elements of mathematics, conceived in this spirit, would constitute a training in logical method together with an acquisition of the precise ideas which lie at the base of the scientific and philosophical investigations of the universe. Would it be easy to continue the excellent reforms in mathematical instruction which this generation has already achieved, so as to include in the curriculum this wider and more philosophic spirit? Frankly, I think that this result would be very hard to achieve as the result of single individual efforts. For reasons which I have already briefly indicated, all reforms in education are very difficult to effect. But the continued pressure of combined effort, provided that the ideal is really present in the minds of the mass of teachers, can do much, and effects in the end surprising modification. Gradually the requisite books get written, still more gradually the examinations are reformed so as to give weight to the less technical aspects of the subject, and then all recent experience has shown that the majority of teachers are only too ready to welcome any practicable means of rescuing the subject from the reproach of being a mechanical discipline.

CHAPTER VII

Universities and Their Function

I

The expansion of universities is one marked feature of the social life in the present age. All countries have shared in this movement, but more especially America, which thereby occupies a position of honour. It is, however, possible to be overwhelmed even by the gifts of good fortune; and this growth of universities, in number of institutions, in size, and in internal complexity of organization, discloses some danger of destroying the very sources of their usefulness, in the absence of a widespread understanding of the primary functions which universities should perform in the service of a nation. These remarks, as to the necessity for reconsideration of the function of universities, apply to all the more developed countries. They are only more especially applicable to America, because this country has taken the lead in a development which, under wise guidance, may prove to be one of the most fortunate forward steps which civilisation has yet taken.

This article will only deal with the most general principles, though the special problems of the various departments in any university are, of course, innumerable. But generalities require illustration, and for this purpose I choose the business school of a university. This choice is dictated by the fact that business schools represent one of the newer developments of university activity. They are also more particularly relevant to the dominant social activities of modern nations, and for that reason are good examples of the way in which the national life should be affected by the activities of

91

its universities. Also at Harvard, where I have the honour to hold office, the new foundation of a business school on a scale amounting to magnificence has just reached its completion.

There is a certain novelty in the provision of such a school of training, on this scale of magnitude, in one of the few leading universities of the world. It marks the culmination of a movement which for many years past has introduced analogous departments throughout American universities. This is a new fact in the university world; and it alone would justify some general reflections upon the purpose of a university education, and upon the proved importance of that purpose for the welfare of the social organism.

The novelty of business schools must not be exaggerated. At no time have universities been restricted to pure abstract learning. The University of Salerno in Italy, the earliest of European universities, was devoted to medicine. In England, at Cambridge, in the year 1316, a college was founded for the special purpose of providing 'clerks for the King's service.' Universities have trained clergy, medical men, lawyers, engineers. Business is now a highly intellectualized vocation, so it well fits into the series. There is, however, this novelty: the curriculum suitable for a business school, and the various modes of activity of such a school, are still in the experimental stage. Hence the peculiar importance of recurrence to general principles in connection with the moulding of these schools. It would, however, be an act of presumption on my part if I were to enter upon any consideration of details, or even upon types of policy affecting the balance of the whole training. Upon such questions I have no special knowledge, and therefore have no word of advice.

II

The universities are schools of education, and schools of research. But the primary reason for their existence is not to be found either in the mere knowledge conveyed to the students or in the mere opportunities for research afforded to the members of the faculty.

Both these functions could be performed at a cheaper rate, apart from these very expensive institutions. Books are cheap, and the system of apprenticeship is well understood. So far as the mere imparting of information is concerned, no university has had any justification for existence since the popularisation of printing in the fifteenth century. Yet the chief impetus to the foundation of universities came after that date, and in more recent times has even increased.

The justification for a university is that it preserves the connection between knowledge and the zest of life, by uniting the young and the old in the imaginative consideration of learning. The university imparts information, but it imparts it imaginatively. At least, this is the function which it should perform for society. A university which fails in this respect has no reason for existence. This atmosphere of excitement, arising from imaginative consideration, transforms knowledge. A fact is no longer a bare fact: it is invested with all its possibilities. It is no longer a burden on the memory: it is energising as the poet of our dreams, and as the architect of our purposes.

Imagination is not to be divorced from the facts: it is a way of illuminating the facts. It works by eliciting the general principles which apply to the facts, as they exist, and then by an intellectual survey of alternative possibilities which are consistent with those principles. It enables men to construct an intellectual vision of a new world, and it preserves the zest of life by the suggestion of satisfying purposes.

Youth is imaginative, and if the imagination be strengthened by discipline this energy of imagination can in great measure be preserved through life. The tragedy of the world is that those who are imaginative have but slight experience, and those who are experienced have feeble imaginations. Fools act on imagination without knowledge; pedants act on knowledge without imagination. The task of a university is to weld together imagination and experience.

The initial discipline of imagination in its period of youthful vigour requires that there be no responsibility for immediate action. The habit of unbiased thought, whereby the ideal variety of exemplification is discerned in its derivation from general principles, cannot be acquired when there is the daily task of preserving a concrete organisation. You must be free to think rightly and wrongly, and free to appreciate the variousness of the universe undisturbed by its perils.

These reflections upon the general functions of a university can be at once translated in terms of the particular functions of a business school. We need not flinch from the assertion that the main function of such a school is to produce men with a greater zest for business. It is a libel upon human nature to conceive that zest for life is the product of pedestrian purposes directed toward the narrow routine of material comforts. Mankind by its pioneering instinct, and in a hundred other ways, proclaims the falsehood of that lie.

In the modern complex social organism, the adventure of life cannot be disjoined from intellectual adventure. Amid simpler circumstances, the pioneer can follow the urge of his instinct, directed toward the scene of his vision from the mountain top. But in the complex organisations of modern business the intellectual adventure of analysis, and of imaginative reconstruction, must precede any successful reorganisation. In a simpler world, business relations were simpler, being based on the immediate contact of man with man and on immediate confrontation with all relevant material circumstances. To-day business organisation requires an imaginative grasp of the psychologies of populations engaged in differing modes of occupation; of populations scattered through cities, through mountains, through plains; of populations on the ocean, and of populations in mines, and of populations in forests. It requires an imaginative grasp of conditions in the tropics, and of conditions in temperate zones. It requires an imaginative grasp of the interlocking interests of great organisations, and of the reactions of the whole complex to any change in one of its elements. It requires an imaginative understanding of laws of political economy, not merely in the abstract, but also with the power to construe them in terms of the particular circumstances of a concrete business. It requires some knowledge of the habits of government, and of the variations of those habits under diverse conditions. It requires an imaginative vision of the binding forces of any human organisation, a sympathetic vision of the limits of human nature and of the conditions which evoke loyalty of service. It requires some knowledge of the laws of health, and of the laws of fatigue, and of the conditions for sustained reliability. It requires an imaginative understanding of the social effects of the conditions of factories. It requires a sufficient conception of the rôle of applied science in modern society. It requires that discipline of character which can say 'yes' and 'no' to other men, not by reason of blind obstinacy, but with firmness derived from a conscious evaluation of relevant alternatives.

The universities have trained the intellectual pioneers of our civilisation—the priests, the lawyers, the statesmen, the doctors, the men of science, and the men of letters. They have been the home of those ideals which lead men to confront the confusion of their present times. The Pilgrim Fathers left England to found a state of society according to the ideals of their religious faith; and one of their earlier acts was the foundation of Harvard University in Cambridge, named after that ancient mother of ideals in England, to which so many of them owed their training. The conduct of business now requires intellectual imagination of the same type as that which in former times has mainly passed into those other occupations; and the universities are the organisations which have supplied this type of mentality for the service of the progress of the European races.

In early mediæval history the origin of universities was obscure and almost unnoticed. They were a gradual and natural growth. But their existence is the reason for the sustained, rapid progressiveness of European life in so many fields of activity. By their agency the adventure of action met the adventure of thought. It would not have been possible antecedently to have divined that such organisations would have been successful. Even now, amid the imperfections of all things human, it is sometimes difficult to understand how they succeed in their work. Of course there is much failure in the work of universities. But, if we take a broad view of history, their success has been remarkable and almost uniform. The cultural histories of Italy, of France, of Germany, of Holland, of Scotland, of England, of the United States, bear witness to the influence of universities. By 'cultural history' I am not chiefly thinking of the lives of scholars; I mean the energising of the lives of those men who gave to France, to Germany, and to other countries that impress of types of human achievement which, by their addition to the zest of life, form the foundation of our patriotism. We love to be members of a society which can do those things.

There is one great difficulty which hampers all the higher types of human endeavour. In modern times this difficulty has even increased in its possibilities for evil. In any large organisation the younger men, who are novices, must be set to jobs which consist in carrying out fixed duties in obedience to orders. No president of a large corporation meets his youngest employee at his office door with the offer of the most responsible job which the work of that corporation includes. The young men are set to work at a fixed routine, and only occasionally even see the president as he passes in and out of the building. Such work is a great discipline. It imparts knowledge, and it produces reliability of character; also it is the only work for which the young men, in that novice stage, are fit, and it is the work for which they are hired. There can be no criticism of the custom, but there may be an unfortunate effect— prolonged routine work dulls the imagination.

The result is that qualities essential at a later stage of a career are apt to be stamped out in an earlier stage. This is only an instance of the more general fact, that necessary technical excellence can only be acquired by a training which is apt to damage those energies of mind which should direct the technical skill. This is the key fact in education, and the reason for most of its difficulties.

The way in which a university should function in the preparation for an intellectual career, such as modern business or one of the older professions, is by promoting the imaginative consideration of the various general principles underlying that career. Its students thus pass into their period of technical apprenticeship with their imaginations already practised in connecting details with general principles. The routine then receives its meaning, and also illumin- ates the principles which give it that meaning. Hence, instead of a drudgery issuing in a blind rule of thumb, the properly trained man has some hope of obtaining an imagination disciplined by detailed facts and by necessary habits.

Thus the proper function of a university is the imaginative acquisition of knowledge. Apart from this importance of the imagination, there is no reason why business men, and other pro- fessional men, should not pick up their facts bit by bit as they want them for particular occasions. A university is imaginative or it is nothing—at least nothing useful.

III

Imagination is a contagious disease. It cannot be measured by the yard, or weighed by the pound, and then delivered to the students by members of the faculty. It can only be communicated by a faculty whose members themselves wear their learning with imagination. In saying this, I am only repeating one of the oldest of observations. More than two thousand years ago the ancients symbolised learning by a torch passing from hand to hand down the generations. That lighted torch is the imagination of which I speak. The whole art in the organisation of a university is the provision of a faculty whose learning is lighted up with imagination. This is the problem of problems in university education; and unless we are careful the recent vast extension of universities in number of students and in variety of activities—of which we are so justly proud—will fail in producing its proper results, by the mishandling of this problem.

The combination of imagination and learning normally requires some leisure, freedom from restraint, freedom from harassing worry, some variety of experiences, and the stimulation of other minds diverse in opinion and diverse in equipment. Also there is required the excitement of curiosity, and the self-confidence derived from pride in the achievements of the surrounding society in procuring the advance of knowledge. Imagination cannot be acquired once and for all, and then kept indefinitely in an ice box to be produced periodically in stated quantities. The learned and imaginative life is a way of living, and is not an article of commerce.

It is in respect to the provision and utilisation of these conditions for an efficient faculty that the two functions of education and research meet together in a university. Do you want your teachers to be imaginative? Then encourage them to research. Do you want your researchers to be imaginative? Then bring them into intellectual sympathy with the young at the most eager, imaginative period of life, when intellects are just entering upon their mature discipline. Make your researchers explain themselves to active minds, plastic and with the world before them; make your young students crown their period of intellectual acquisition by some contact with minds gifted with experience of intellectual adventure.

Education is discipline for the adventure of life; research is intellectual adventure; and the universities should be homes of adventure shared in common by young and old. For successful education there must always be a certain freshness in the knowledge dealt with. It must either be new in itself or it must be invested with some novelty of application to the new world of new times. Knowledge does not keep any better than fish. You may be dealing with knowledge of the old species, with some old truth; but somehow or other it must come to the students, as it were, just drawn out of the sea and with the freshness of its immediate importance.

It is the function of the scholar to evoke into life wisdom and beauty which, apart from his magic, would remain lost in the past. A progressive society depends upon its inclusion of three groups— scholars, discoverers, inventors. Its progress also depends upon the fact that its educated masses are composed of members each with a tinge of scholarship, a tinge of discovery, and a tinge of invention. I am here using the term 'discovery' to mean the progress of knowledge in respect to truths of some high generality, and the term 'invention' to mean the progress of knowledge in respect to the application of general truths in particular ways subservient to present needs. It is evident that these three groups merge into each other, and also that men engaged in practical affairs are properly to be called inventors so far as they contribute to the progress of society. But any one individual has his own limitation of function, and his own peculiar needs. What is important for a nation is that there shall be a very close relation between all types of its progressive elements, so that the study may influence the market place, and the market place the study. Universities are the chief agencies for this fusion of progressive activities into an effective instrument of progress. Of course they are not the only agencies, but it is a fact that to-day the progressive nations are those in which universities flourish.

It must not be supposed that the output of a university in the form of original ideas is solely to be measured by printed papers and books labeled with the names of their authors. Mankind is as individual in its mode of output as in the substance of its thoughts. For some of the most fertile minds composition in writing, or in a form reducible to writing, seems to be an impossibility. In every faculty you will find that some of the more brilliant teachers are not among those who publish. Their originality requires for its expression direct intercourse with their pupils in the form of lectures, or of personal discussion. Such men exercise an immense influence; and yet, after the generation of their pupils has passed away, they sleep among the innumerable unthanked benefactors of humanity. Fortunately, one of them is immortal—Socrates.

Thus it would be the greatest mistake to estimate the value of each member of a faculty by the printed work signed with his name. There is at the present day some tendency to fall into this error; and an emphatic protest is necessary against an attitude on the part of authorities which is damaging to efficiency and unjust to unselfish zeal.

But, when all such allowances have been made, one good test for the general efficiency of a faculty is that as a whole it shall be producing in published form its quota of contributions of thought. Such a quota is to be estimated in weight of thought, and not in number of words.

This survey shows that the management of a university faculty has no analogy to that of a business organisation. The public opinion of the faculty, and a common zeal for the purposes of the university, form the only effective safeguards for the high level of university work. The faculty should be a band of scholars, stimulating each other, and freely determining their various activities. You can secure certain formal requirements, that lectures are given at stated times and that instructors and students are in attendance. But the heart of the matter lies beyond all regulation.

The question of justice to the teachers has very little to do with the case. It is perfectly just to hire a man to perform any legal services under any legal conditions as to times and salary. No one need accept the post unless he so desires.

The sole question is, What sort of conditions will produce the type of faculty which will run a successful university? The danger is that it is quite easy to produce a faculty entirely unfit—a faculty of very efficient pedants and dullards. The general public will only detect the difference after the university has stunted the promise of youth for scores of years.

The modern university system in the great democratic countries will only be successful if the ultimate authorities exercise singular restraint, so as to remember that universities cannot be dealt with according to the rules and policies which apply to the familiar business corporations. Business schools are no exception to this law of university life. There is really nothing to add to what the presidents of many American universities have recently said in public on this topic. But whether the effective portion of the general public, in America or other countries, will follow their advice appears to be doubtful. The whole point of a university, on its educational side, is to bring the young under the intellectual influence of a band of imaginative scholars. There can be no escape from proper attention to the conditions which—as experience has shown—will produce such a band.

I V

The two premier universities of Europe, in age and in dignity, are the University of Paris and the University of Oxford. I will speak of my own country because I know it best. The University of Oxford may have sinned in many ways. But, for all her deficiencies, she has throughout the ages preserved one supreme merit, beside which all failures in detail are as dust in the balance: for century after century, throughout the long course of her existence, she has produced bands of scholars who treated learning imaginatively. For that service alone, no one who loves culture can think of her without emotion.

But it is quite unnecessary for me to cross the ocean for my examples. The author of the Declaration of Independence, Mr. Jefferson, has some claim to be the greatest American. The perfection of his various achievements certainly places him among the few great men of all ages. He founded a university, and devoted one side of his complex genius to placing that university amid every circumstance which could stimulate the imagination—beauty of buildings, of situation, and every other stimulation of equipment and organisation.

There are many other universities in America which can point my moral, but my final example shall be Harvard—the representative university of the Puritan movement. The New England

Puritans of the seventeenth and eighteenth centuries were the most intensely imaginative people, restrained in their outward expression, and fearful of symbolism by physical beauty, but, as it were, racked with the intensity of spiritual truths intellectually imagined. The Puritan faculties of those centuries must have been imaginative indeed, and they produced great men whose names have gone round the world. In later times Puritanism softened, and, in the golden age of literary New England, Emerson, Lowell, and Longfellow set their mark upon Harvard. The modern scientific age then gradually supervenes, and again in William James we find the typical imaginative scholar.

To-day business comes to Harvard; and the gift which the University has to offer is the old one of imagination, the lighted torch which passes from hand to hand. It is a dangerous gift, which has started many a conflagration. If we are timid as to that danger, the proper course is to shut down our universities. Imagination is a gift which has often been associated with great commercial peoples—with Greece, with Florence, with Venice, with the learning of Holland, and with the poetry of England. Commerce and imagination thrive together. It is a gift which all must pray for their country who desire for it that abiding greatness achieved by Athens: —

> Her citizens, imperial spirits,
> Rule the present from the past.

For American education no smaller ideal can suffice.

CHAPTER VIII

The Organisation of Thought

The subject of this address is the organisation of thought, a topic evidently capable of many diverse modes of treatment. I intend more particularly to give some account of that department of logical science with which some of my own studies have been connected. But I am anxious, if I can succeed in so doing, to handle this account so as to exhibit the relation with certain considerations which underlie general scientific activities.

It is no accident that an age of science has developed into an age of organisation. Organised thought is the basis of organised action. Organisation is the adjustment of diverse elements so that their mutual relations may exhibit some predetermined quality. An epic poem is a triumph of organisation, that is to say, it is a triumph in the unlikely event of its being a good epic poem. It is the successful organisation of multitudinous sounds of words, associations of words, pictorial memories of diverse events and feelings ordinarily occurring in life, combined with a special narrative of great events: the whole so disposed as to excite emotions which, as defined by Milton, are simple, sensuous, and passionate. The number of successful epic poems is commensurate, or rather, is inversely commensurate, with the obvious difficulty of the task of organisation.

Science is the organisation of thought. But the example of the epic poem warns us that science is not any organisation of thought. It is an organisation of a certain definite type which we will endeavour to determine.

Science is a river with two sources, the practical source and the theoretical source. The practical source is the desire to direct our actions to achieve predetermined ends. For example, the British nation, fighting for justice, turns to science, which teaches it the importance of compounds of nitrogen. The theoretical source is the desire to understand. Now I am going to emphasise the importance of theory in science. But to avoid misconception I most emphatically state that I do not consider one source as in any sense nobler than the other, or intrinsically more interesting. I cannot see why it is nobler to strive to understand than to busy oneself with the right ordering of one's actions. Both have their bad sides; there are evil ends directing actions, and there are ignoble curiosities of the understanding.

The importance, even in practice, of the theoretical side of science arises from the fact that action must be immediate, and takes place under circumstances which are excessively complicated. If we wait for the necessities of action before we commence to arrange our ideas, in peace we shall have lost our trade, and in war we shall have lost the battle. Success in practice depends on theorists who, led by other motives of exploration, have been there before, and by some good chance have hit upon the relevant ideas. By a theorist I do not mean a man who is up in the clouds, but a man whose motive for thought is the desire to formulate correctly the rules according to which events occur. A successful theorist should be excessively interested in immediate events, otherwise he is not at all likely to formulate correctly anything about them. Of course, both sources of science exist in all men.

Now, what is this thought organisation which we call science? The first aspect of modern science which struck thoughtful observers was its inductive character. The nature of induction, its importance, and the rules of inductive logic have been considered by a long series of thinkers, especially English thinkers: Bacon, Herschel, J. S. Mill, Venn, Jevons, and others. I am not going to plunge into an analysis of the process of induction. Induction is the machinery and not the product, and it is the product which I want to consider. When we understand the product we shall be in a stronger position to improve the machinery.

First, there is one point which it is necessary to emphasise. There is a tendency in analysing scientific processes to assume a given assemblage of concepts applying to nature, and to imagine that the discovery of laws of nature consists in selecting by means of inductive logic some one out of a definite set of possible alternative relations which may hold between the things in nature answering to these obvious concepts. In a sense this assumption is fairly correct, especially in regard to the earlier stages of science. Mankind found itself in possession of certain concepts respecting nature—for example, the concept of fairly permanent material bodies—and proceeded to determine laws which related the corresponding percepts in nature. But the formulation of laws changed the concepts, sometimes gently by an added precision, sometimes violently. At first this process was not much noticed, or at least was felt to be a process curbed within narrow bounds, not touching fundamental ideas. At the stage where we now are, the formulation of the concepts can be seen to be as important as the formulation of the empirical laws connecting the events in the universe as thus conceived by us. For example, the concepts of life, of heredity, of a material body, of a molecule, of an atom, of an electron, of energy, of space, of time, of quantity, and of number. I am not dogmatising about the best way of getting such ideas straight. Certainly it will only be done by those who have devoted themselves to a special study of the facts in question. Success is never absolute, and progress in the right direction is the result of a slow, gradual process of continual comparison of ideas with facts. The criterion of success is that we should be able to formulate empirical laws, that is, statements of relations, connecting the various parts of the universe as thus conceived, laws with the property that we can interpret the actual events of our lives as being our fragmentary knowledge of this conceived interrelated whole.

But, for the purpose of science, what is the actual world? Has science to wait for the termination of the metaphysical debate till it can determine its own subject-matter? I suggest that science has a much more homely starting-ground. Its task is the discovery of the relations which exist within that flux of perceptions, sensations, and emotions which forms our experience of life. The panorama yielded by sight, sound, taste, smell, touch, and by more inchoate sensible feelings, is the sole field of activity. It is in this way that science is the thought organisation of experience. The most obvious aspect of this field of actual experience is its disorderly character. It is for each person a *continuum*, fragmentary, and with elements not clearly differentiated. The comparison of the sensible experiences of diverse people brings its own difficulties. I insist on the radically untidy, ill-adjusted character of the fields of actual experience from which science starts. To grasp this fundamental truth is the first step in wisdom, when constructing a philosophy of science. This fact is concealed by the influence of language, moulded by science, which foists on us exact concepts as though they represented the immediate deliverances of experience. The result is, that we imagine that we have immediate experience of a world of perfectly defined objects implicated in perfectly defined events which, as known to us by the direct deliverance of our senses, happen at exact instants of time, in a space formed by exact points, without parts and without magnitude: the neat, trim, tidy, exact world which is the goal of scientific thought.

My contention is, that this world is a world of ideas, and that its internal relations are relations between abstract concepts, and that the elucidation of the precise connection between this world and the feelings of actual experience is the fundamental question of scientific philosophy. The question which I am inviting you to consider is this: How does exact thought apply to the fragmentary, vague *continua* of experience? I am not saying that it does not apply: quite the contrary. But I want to know how it applies. The solution I am asking for is not a phrase, however brilliant, but a solid branch of science, constructed with slow patience, showing in detail how the correspondence is effected.

The first great steps in the organisation of thought were due exclusively to the practical source of scientific activity, without any admixture of theoretical impulse. Their slow accomplishment was the cause and also the effect of the gradual evolution of moderately rational beings. I mean the formation of the concepts of definite material objects, of the determinate lapse of time, of simultaneity, of recurrence, of definite relative position, and of analogous fundamental ideas, according to which the flux of our experience is mentally arranged for handy reference: in fact, the whole apparatus of commonsense thought. Consider in your mind some definite chair. The concept of that chair is simply the concept of all the interrelated experiences connected with that chair—namely, of the experience of the folk who made it, of the folk who sold it, of the folk who have seen it or used it, of the man who is now experiencing a comfortable sense of support, combined with our expectations of an analogous future, terminated finally by a different set of experiences when the chair collapses and becomes firewood. The formation of that type of concept was a tremendous job, and zoologists and geologists tell us that it took many tens of millions of years. I can well believe it.

I now emphasise two points. In the first place, science is rooted in what I have just called the whole apparatus of commonsense thought. That is the *datum* from which it starts, and to which it must recur. We may speculate, if it amuses us, on other beings in other planets who have arranged analogous experiences according to an entirely different conceptual code—namely, who have directed their chief attention to different relations between their various experiences. But the task is too complex, too gigantic, to be revised in its main outlines. You may polish up commonsense, you may contradict in detail, you may surprise it. But ultimately your whole task is to satisfy it.

In the second place, neither commonsense nor science can proceed with their task of thought organisation without departing in some respect from the strict consideration of what is actual in experience. Think again of the chair. Among the experiences upon which its concept is based, I included our expectations of its future history. I should have gone further and included our imagination of all the possible experiences which in ordinary language we should call perceptions of the chair which might have occurred. This is a difficult question, and I do not see my way through it. But, at present, in the construction of a theory of space and of time there seem insuperable difficulties if we refuse to admit ideal experiences.

This imaginative perception of experiences, which, if they occurred, would be coherent with our actual experiences, seems fundamental in our lives. It is neither wholly arbitrary, nor yet fully determined. It is a vague background which is only made in part definite by isolated activities of thought. Consider, for example, our thoughts of the unseen flora of Brazil.

Ideal experiences are closely connected with our imaginative reproduction of the actual experiences of other people, and also with our almost inevitable conception of ourselves as receiving our impressions from an external complex reality beyond ourselves. It may be that an adequate analysis of every source and every type of experience yields demonstrative proof of such a reality and of its nature. Indeed, it is hardly to be doubted that this is the case. The precise elucidation of this question is the problem of metaphysics. One of the points which I am urging in this address is, that the basis of science does not depend on the assumption of any of the conclusions of metaphysics; but that both science and metaphysics start from the same given groundwork of immediate experience, and in the main proceed in opposite directions on their diverse tasks.

For example, metaphysics inquires how our perceptions of the chair relate us to some true reality. Science gathers up these perceptions into a determinate class, adds to them ideal perceptions of analogous sort, which under assignable circumstances would be obtained, and this single concept of that set of perceptions is all that science needs.

My immediate problem is to inquire into the nature of the texture of science. Science is essentially logical. The nexus between its concepts is a logical nexus, and the grounds for its detailed assertions are logical grounds. King James said, "No bishops, no king." With greater confidence we can say, "No logic, no science." The reason for the instinctive dislike which most men of science feel towards the recognition of this truth is, I think, the barren failure of logical theory during the past three or four centuries. We may trace this failure back to the worship of authority, which in some respects increased in the learned world at the time of the Renaissance. Mankind then changed its authority, and this fact temporally acted as an emancipation. But the main fact, and we can find complaints[1] of it at the very commencement of the modern movement, was the establishment of a reverential attitude towards any statement made by a classical author. Scholars became commentators on truths too fragile to bear translation. A science which hesitates to forget its founders is lost. To this hesitation I ascribe the barrenness of logic. Another reason for distrust of logical theory and of mathematics is

[1] *E.g.* in 1551 by Italian schoolmen; cf. Scarpi's *History of the Council of Trent,* under that date.

the belief that deductive reasoning can give you nothing new. Your conclusions are contained in your premises, which by hypothesis are known to you.

In the first place this last condemnation of logic neglects the fragmentary, disconnected character of human knowledge. To know one premise on Monday, and another premise on Tuesday, is useless to you on Wednesday. Science is a permanent record of premises, deductions, and conclusions, verified all along the line by its correspondence with facts. Secondly, it is untrue that when we know the premises we also know the conclusions. In arithmetic, for example, mankind are not calculating boys. Any theory which proves that they are conversant with the consequences of their assumptions must be wrong. We can imagine beings who possess such insight. But we are not such creatures. Both these answers are, I think, true and relevant. But they are not satisfactory. They are too much in the nature of bludgeons, too external. We want something more explanatory of the very real difficulty which the question suggests. In fact, the true answer is embedded in the discussion of our main problem of the relation of logic to natural science.

It will be necessary to sketch in broad outline some relevant features of modern logic. In doing so I shall try to avoid the profound general discussions and the minute technical classifications which occupy the main part of traditional logic. It is characteristic of a science in its earlier stages—and logic has become fossilised in such a stage—to be both ambitiously profound in its aims and trivial in its handling of details.

We can discern four departments of logical theory. By an analogy which is not so very remote I will call these departments or sections the arithmetic section, the algebraic section, the section of general-function theory, the analytical section. I do not mean that arithmetic arises in the first section, algebra in the second section, and so on; but the names are suggestive of certain qualities of thought in each section which are reminiscent of analogous qualities in arithmetic, in algebra, in the general theory of a mathematical function, and in the mathematical analysis of the properties of particular functions.

The first section—namely, the arithmetic stage—deals with the relations of definite propositions to each other, just as arithmetic deals with definite numbers. Consider any definite proposition; call it *"p."* We conceive that there is always another proposition which is the direct contradictory to *"p"*; call it "not-*p*." When we have got two propositions, *p* and *q*, we can form derivative propositions from them, and from their contradictories. We can say, "At last one of *p* or *q* is true, and perhaps both." Let us call this proposition *"p* or *q."* I may mention as an aside that one of the greatest living philosophers has stated that this use of the word "or"—namely, *"p* or *q"* in the sense that either or both may be true—makes him despair of exact expression. We must brave his wrath, which is unintelligible to me.

We have thus got hold of four new propositions, namely, *"p* or *q,"* and "not-*p* or *q,"* and *"p* or not-*q,"* and "not-*p* or not-*q."* Call these the set of disjunctive derivatives. There are, so far, in all eight propositions, *p*, not-*p*, *q*, not-*q*, and the four disjunctive derivatives. Any pair of these eight propositions can be taken, and substituted for *p* and *q* in the foregoing treatment. Thus each pair yields eight propositions, some of which may have been obtained before. By proceeding in this way we arrive at an unending set of propositions of growing complexity, ultimately derived from the two original propositions *p* or *q*. Of course, only a few are important. Similarly we can start from three propositions, *p*, *q*, *r*, or from four propositions, *p*, *q*, *r*, *s*, and so on. Any one of the propositions of these aggregates may be true or false. It has no other alternative. Whichever it is, true or false, call it the "truth-value" of the proposition.

The first section of logical inquiry is to settle what we know of the truth-values of these propositions, when we know the truth-values of some of them. The inquiry, so far as it is worth while carrying it, is not very abstruse, and the best way of expressing its results is a detail which I will not now consider. This inquiry forms the arithmetic stage.

The next section of logic is the algebraic stage. Now, the difference between arithmetic and algebra is, that in arithmetic definite numbers are considered, and in algebra symbols—namely, letters—are introduced which stand for any numbers. The idea of a number is also enlarged. These letters, standing for any numbers, are called sometimes variables and sometimes parameters. Their essential characteristic is that they are undetermined, unless, indeed, the algebraic conditions which they satisfy implicitly determine them. Then they are sometimes called unknowns. An algebraic formula with letters is a blank form. It becomes a determinate arithmetic statement when definite numbers are substituted for the letters. The importance of algebra is a tribute to the study of form. Consider now the following proposition—

The specific heat of mercury is 0·033.

This is a definite proposition which, with certain limitations, is true. But the truth-value of the proposition does not immediately concern us. Instead of mercury put a mere letter which is the name of some undetermined thing: we get—

The specific heat of x is 0·033.

This is not a proposition; it has been called by Russell a propositional function. It is the logical analogy of an algebraic expression. Let us write $f(x)$ for any propositional function. We could also generalise still further, and say,

The specific heat of x is y.

We thus get another propositional function, $F(x, y)$, of two arguments x and y, and so on for any number of arguments.

Now, consider $f(x)$. There is the range of values of x, for which $f(x)$ is a proposition, true or false. For values of x outside this range, $f(x)$ is not a proposition at all, and is neither true nor false. It may have vague suggestion for us, but it has no unit meaning of definite assertion. For example,

The specific heat of water is 0·033

is a proposition which is false; and—

The specific heat of virtue is 0·033

is, I should imagine, not a proposition at all; so that it is neither true nor false, though its component parts raise various associations in our minds. This range of values, for which $f(x)$ has sense, is called the "type" of the argument x.

But there is also a range of values of x for which $f(x)$ is a true proposition. This is the class of those values of the argument which *satisfy* $f(x)$. This class may have no members, or, in the other extreme, the class may be the whole type of the arguments.

We thus conceive two general propositions respecting the indefinite number of propositions which share in the same logical form, that is, which are values of the same propositional function. One of these propositions is,

$f(x)$ yields a true proposition for each value
of x of the proper type;

the other proposition is,

There is a value of x for which $f(x)$ is true.

Given two, or more, propositional functions $f(x)$ and $\varphi(x)$ with the same argument x, we form derivative propositional functions, namely,

$f(x)$ or $\varphi(x)$, $f(x)$ or not-$\varphi(x)$,

and so on with the contradictories, obtaining, as in the arithmetical stage, an unending aggregate of propositional functions. Also each propositional function yields two general propositions. The theory of the interconnection between the truth-values of the general propositions arising from any such aggregate of propositional functions forms a simple and elegant chapter of mathematical logic.

In this algebraic section of logic the theory of types crops up, as we have already noted. It cannot be neglected without the introduction of error. Its theory has to be settled at least by some safe hypothesis, even if it does not go to the philosophic basis of the question. This part of the subject is obscure and difficult, and has not been finally elucidated, though Russell's brilliant work has opened out the subject.

The final impulse to modern logic comes from the independent discovery of the importance of the logic variable by Frege and Peano. Frege went further than Peano, but by an unfortunate symbolism rendered his work so obscure that no one fully recognised his meaning who had not found it out for himself. But the movement has a large history reaching back to Leibniz and even to Aristotle. Among English contributors are De Morgan, Boole, and Sir Alfred Kempe; their work is of the first rank.

The third logical section is the stage of general-function theory. In logical language, we perform in this stage the transition from intension to extension, and investigate the theory of denotation. Take the propositional function $f(x)$. There is the class, or range of values for x, whose members satisfy $f(x)$. But the same range may be the class whose members satisfy another propositional function $\varphi(x)$. It is necessary to investigate how to indicate the class by a way which is indifferent as between the various propositional functions which are satisfied by any member of it, and of it only. What has to be done is to analyse the nature of propositions about a class—namely, those propositions whose truth-values depend on the class itself and not on the particular meaning by which the class is indicated.

Furthermore, there are propositions about alleged individuals indicated by descriptive phrases: for example, propositions about "the present King of England," who does exist, and "the present Emperor of Brazil," who does not exist. More complicated, but analogous, questions involving propositional functions of two variables involve the notion of "correlation," just as functions of one argument involve classes. Similarly functions of three arguments yield three-cornered correlations, and so on. This logical section is one Russell has made peculiarly his own by work which must always remain fundamental. I have called this the section of functional theory, because its ideas are essential to the construction of logical denoting functions which include as a special case ordinary mathematical functions, such as sine, logarithm, etc. In each of these three stages it will be necessary gradually to introduce an appropriate symbolism, if we are to pass on to the fourth stage.

The fourth logical section, the analytic stage, is concerned with the investigation of the properties of special logical constructions, that is, of classes and correlations of special sorts. The whole of mathematics is included here. So the section is a large one. In fact, it is mathematics, neither more nor less, but it includes an analysis of mathematical ideas not hitherto included in the scope of that science, nor, indeed, contemplated at all. The essence of this stage is construction. It is by means of suitable constructions that the great framework of applied mathematics, comprising the theories of number, quantity, time, and space, is elaborated.

It is impossible, even in brief outline, to explain how mathematics is developed from the concepts of class and correlation, including many-cornered correlations, which are established in the third section. I can only allude to the headings of the process, which is fully developed in the work, *Principia Mathematica,* by Mr. Russell and myself. There are in this process of development seven special sorts of correlations which are of peculiar interest. The first sort comprises one-to-many, many-to-one, and one-to-one correlations. The second sort comprises serial relations, that is, correlations by which the members of some field are arranged in serial order, so that, in the sense defined by the relation, any member of the field is either before or after any other member. The third class comprises inductive relations, that is, correlations on which the theory of mathematical induction depends. The fourth class comprises selective relations, which are required for the general theory of arithmetic operations, and elsewhere. It is in connection with such relations that the famous multiplicative axiom arises for consideration. The fifth class comprises vector relations, from which the theory of quantity arises. The sixth class comprises ratio relations, which interconnect number and quantity. The seventh class comprises three-cornered and four-cornered relations which occur in geometry.

A bare enumeration of technical names, such as the above, is not very illuminating, though it may help to a comprehension of the demarcations of the subject. Please remember that the names are technical names, meant, no doubt, to be suggestive, but used in strictly defined senses. We have suffered much from critics who consider it sufficient to criticise our procedure on the slender basis of a knowledge of the dictionary meanings of such terms. For example, a one-to-one correlation depends on the notion of a class with only one member, and this notion is defined without appeal to the concept of the number one. The notion of diversity is all that is wanted. Thus the class α has only one member, if (1) the class of values of x which satisfies the propositional function,

$$x \text{ is not a member of } \alpha,$$

is not the whole type of relevant values of x, and if (2) the propositional function,

x and y are members of of α, and x is diverse from y

is false, whatever be the values of x and y in the relevant type.

Analogous procedures are obviously possible for higher finite cardinal members. Thus, step by step, the whole cycle of current mathematical ideas is capable of logical definition. The process is detailed and laborious, and, like all science, knows nothing of a royal road of airy phrases. The essence of the process is, first, to construct the notion in terms of the forms of propositions, that is, in terms of the relevant propositional functions, and secondly, to prove the fundamental truths which hold about the notion by reference to the results obtained in the algebraic section of logic.

It will be seen that in this process the whole apparatus of special indefinable mathematical concepts, and special *a priori* mathematical premises, respecting number, quantity, and space, has vanished. Mathematics is merely an apparatus for analysing the deductions which can be drawn from any particular premises, supplied by commonsense, or by more refined scientific observation, so far as these deductions depend on the forms of the propositions. Propositions of certain forms are continually occurring in thought. Our existing mathematics is the analysis of deductions which concern those forms and in some way are important, either from practical utility or theoretical interest. Here I am speaking of the science as it in fact exists. A theoretical definition of mathematics must include in its scope any deductions depending on the mere forms of propositions. But, of course no one would wish to develop that part of mathematics which in no sense is of importance.

This hasty summary of logical ideas suggests some reflections. The question arises, How many forms of propositions are there? The answer is, An unending number. The reason for the supposed sterility of logical science can thus be discerned. Aristotle founded the science by conceiving the idea of the form of a proposition, and by conceiving deduction as taking place in virtue of the forms. But he confined propositions to four forms, now named A, I, E, O. So long as logicians were obsessed by this unfortunate restriction, real progress was impossible. Again, in their theory of form, both Aristotle and subsequent logicians came very near to the theory of the logical variable. But to come very near to a true theory, and to grasp its precise application, are two very different things, as the history of science teaches us. Everything of importance has been said before by somebody who did not discover it.

Again, one reason why logical deductions are not obvious is, that logical form is not a subject which ordinarily enters into thought. Commonsense deduction probably moves by blind instinct from concrete proposition to concrete proposition, guided by some habitual association of ideas. Thus commonsense fails in the presence of a wealth of material.

A more important question is the relation of induction, based on observation, to deductive logic. There is a tradition of opposition between adherents of induction and of deduction. In my view, it would be just as sensible for the two ends of a worm to quarrel. Both observation and deduction are necessary for any knowledge worth having. We cannot get at an inductive law without having recourse to a propositional function. For example, take the statement of observed fact,

This body is mercury, and its specific heat is 0·033.

The propositional function is formed,

Either x is not mercury, or its specific heat is 0·033.

The inductive law is the assumption of the truth of the general proposition, that the above propositional function is true for every value of x in the relevant type.

But it is objected that this process and its consequences are so simple that an elaborate science is out of place. In the same way, a British sailor knows the salt sea when he sails over it. What, then, is the use of an elaborate chemical analysis of sea-water? There is the general answer, that you cannot know too much of methods which you always employ; and there is the special answer, that logical forms and logical implications are not so very simple, and that the whole of mathematics is evidence to this effect.

One great use of the study of logical method is not in the region of elaborate deduction, but to guide us in the study of the formation of the main concepts of science. Consider geometry, for example. What are the points which compose space? Euclid tells us that they are without parts and without magnitude. But how is the notion of a point derived from the sense-perceptions from which science starts? Certainly points are not direct deliverances of the senses. Here and there we may see or unpleasantly feel something suggestive of a point. But this is a rare phenomenon, and certainly does not warrant the conception of space as composed of points. Our knowledge of space properties is not based on any observations of relations between points. It arises from experience of relations between bodies. Now a fundamental space-relation between bodies is that one body may be part of another. We are tempted to define the "whole and part" relation by saying that the points occupied by the part are some of the points occupied by the whole. But "whole and part" being more fundamental than the notion of "point," this definition is really circular and vicious.

We accordingly ask whether any other definition of "spatial whole and part" can be given. I think that it can be done in this way, though, if I be mistaken, it is unessential to my general argument. We have come to the conclusion that an extended body is nothing else than the class of perception of it by all its percipients, actual or ideal. Of course, it is not any class of perceptions, but a certain definite sort of class which I have not defined here, except by the vicious method of saying that they are perceptions of body. Now, the perceptions of a part of a body are among the perceptions which compose the whole body. Thus two bodies a and b are both classes of perceptions; and b is part of a when the class which is b is contained in the class which is a. It immediately follows from the logical form of this definition that if b is part of a, and c is part of b, then c is part of a. Thus the relation "whole to part" is transitive. Again, it will be convenient to allow that a body is part of itself. This is a mere question of how you draw the definition. With this understanding, the relation is reflexive. Finally, if a is part of b, and b is part of a, then a and b must be identical. These properties of "whole and part" are not fresh assumptions, they follow from the logical form of our definition.

One assumption has to be made if we assume the ideal infinite divisibility of space. Namely, we assume that every class of perceptions which is an extended body contains other classes of perceptions which are extended bodies diverse from itself. This assumption makes rather a large draft on the theory of ideal perceptions.

Geometry vanishes unless in some form you make it. The assumption is not peculiar to my exposition.

It is then possible to define what we mean by a point. A point is the class of extended objects which, in ordinary language, contain that point. The definition, without presupposing the idea of a point, is rather elaborate, and I have not now time for its statement.

The advantage of introducing points into geometry is the simplicity of the logical expression of their mutual relations. For science, simplicity of definition is of slight importance, but simplicity of mutual relations is essential. Another example of this law is the way physicists and chemists have dissolved the simple idea of an extended body, say of a chair, which a child understands, into a bewildering notion of a complex dance of molecules and atoms and electrons and waves of light. They have thereby gained notions with simpler logical relations.

Space as thus conceived is the exact formulation of the properties of the apparent space of the commonsense world of experience. It is not necessarily the best mode of conceiving the space of the physicist. The one essential requisite is that the correspondence between the commonsense world in its and the physicists' world in its space should be definite and reciprocal.

I will now break off the exposition of the function of logic in connection with the science of natural phenomena. I have endeavoured to exhibit it as the organising principle, analysing the derivation of the concepts from the immediate phenomena, examining the structure of the general propositions which are the assumed laws of nature, establishing their relations to each other in respect to reciprocal implications, deducing the phenomena we may expect under given circumstances.

Logic, properly used, does not shackle thought. It gives freedom, and above all, boldness. Illogical thought hesitates to draw conclusions, because it never knows either what it means, or what it assumes, or how far it trusts its own assumptions, or what will be the effect of any modification of assumptions. Also the mind untrained in that part of constructive logic which is relevant to the subject in hand will be ignorant of the sort of conclusions which follow from various sorts of assumptions, and will be correspondingly dull in divining the inductive laws. The fundamental training in this relevant logic is, undoubtedly, to ponder with an active mind over the known facts of the case, directly observed. But where elaborate deductions are possible, this mental activity requires for its full exercise the direct study of the abstract logical relations. This is applied mathematics.

Neither logic without observation, nor observation without logic, can move one step in the formation of science. We may conceive humanity as engaged in an internecine conflict between youth and age. Youth is not defined by years but by the creative impulse to make something. The aged are those who, before all things, desire not to make a mistake. Logic is the olive branch from the old to the young, the wand which in the hands of youth has the magic property of creating science.

CHAPTER IX

The Anatomy of Some Scientific Ideas

1. Fact

The characteristic of physical science is, that it ignores all judgments of value: for example, æsthetic or moral judgments. It is purely matter-of-fact, and this is the sense in which we must interpret the sonorous phrase, "Man, the servant and the minister of Nature."

The sphere of thought which is thus left is even then too wide for physical science. It would include Ontology, namely, the determination of the nature of what truly exists; in other words, Metaphysics. From an abstract point of view this exclusion of metaphysical inquiry is a pity. Such an inquiry is a necessary critique of the worth of science, to tell us what it all comes to. The reasons for its careful separation from scientific thought are purely practical; namely, because we can agree about science—after due debate—whereas in respect to metaphysics debate has hitherto accentuated disagreement. These characteristics of science and metaphysics were unexpected in the early days of civilised thought. The Greeks thought that metaphysics was easier than physics, and tended to deduce scientific principles from *a priori* conceptions of the nature of things. They were restrained in this disastrous tendency by their vivid naturalism, their delight in first-hand perception. Mediæval Europe shared the tendency without the restraint. It is possible that some distant generations may arrive at unanimous conclusions on ontological questions, whereas scientific progress may have led to ingrained opposing veins of thought which can neither be reconciled

121

nor abandoned. In such times metaphysics and physical science will exchange their rôles. Meanwhile we must take the case as we find it.

But a problem remains. How can mankind agree about science without a preliminary determination of what really is? The answer must be found in an analysis of the facts which form the field of scientific activity. Mankind perceives, and finds itself thinking about its perceptions. It is the thought that matters and not that element of perception which is not thought. When the immediate judgment has been formed—Hullo, red!—it does not matter if we can imagine that in other circumstances—in better circumstances, perhaps—the judgment would have been—Hullo, blue!—or even—Hullo, nothing! For all intents and purposes, at the time it was red. Everything else is hypothetical reconstruction. The field of physical science is composed of these primary thoughts, and of thoughts about these thoughts.

But—to avoid confusion—a false simplicity has been introduced above into the example given of a primary perceptive thought. "Hullo, red!" is not really a primary perceptive thought, though it often is the first thought which finds verbal expression even silently in the mind. Nothing is in isolation. The perception of red is of a red object in its relations to the whole content of the perceiving consciousness.

Among the most easily analysed of such relations are the space relations. Again the red object is in immediate perception nothing else than a red object. It is better termed an "object of redness." Thus a better approximation to an immediate perceptive judgment is, "Hullo, object of redness there!" But, of course, in this formulation other more complex relations are omitted.

This tendency towards a false simplicity in scientific analysis, to an excessive abstraction, to an over-universalising of universals, is derived from the earlier metaphysical stage. It arises from the implicit belief that we are endeavouring to qualify the real with appropriate adjectives. In conformity with this tendency we think, "this real thing is red." Whereas our true goal is to make explicit our perception of the apparent in terms of its relations. What we perceive is redness related to other apparents. Our object is the analysis of the relations.

One aim of science is the harmony of thought, that is, to secure that judgments which are logical contraries should not be thought-expressions of consciousness. Another aim is the extension of such harmonised thought.

Some thoughts arise directly from sense-presentation, and are part of the state of consciousness which is perception. Such a thought is, "An object of redness is there." But in general the thought is not verbal, but is a direct apprehension of qualities and relations within the content of consciousness.

Amid such thoughts there can be no lack of harmony. For direct apprehension is in its essence unique, and it is impossible to apprehend an object as both red and blue. Subsequently it may be judged that if other elements of the consciousness had been different, the apprehension would have been of a blue object. Then—under certain circumstances—the original apprehension will be called an error. But for all that the fact remains, there was an apprehension of a red object.

When we speak of sense-presentation, we mean these primary thoughts essentially involved in its perception. But there are thoughts about thoughts, and thoughts derived from other thoughts. These are secondary thoughts. At this point it is well explicitly to discriminate between an actual thought-expression, namely, a judgment actually made, and a mere proposition which is a hypothetical thought-expression, namely, an imagined possibility of thought-expression. Note that the actual complete thought-content of the consciousness is explicitly neither affirmed nor denied. It is just what *is* thought. Thus, to think "two and two make four" is distinct from affirming that two and two make four. In the first case the proposition is the thought-expression, in the second case the affirmation of the proposition is the thought-expression, and the proposition has been degraded to a mere proposition, namely, to a hypothetical thought-expression which is reflected upon.

A distinction is sometimes made between facts and thoughts. So far as physical science is concerned, the facts are thoughts, and thoughts are facts. Namely, the facts of sense-presentation as they affect science are those elements in the immediate apprehensions which are thoughts. Also, actual thought-expressions, primary or secondary, are the material facts which science interprets.

The distinction that facts are given, but thoughts are free, is not absolute. We can select and modify our sense-presentation, so that facts—in the narrower sense of immediate apprehension of sense-presentation—are to some degree subject to volition. Again, our stream of thought-expression is only partially modified by explicit volition. We can choose our physical experience, and we find ourselves thinking; namely, on the one hand there is selection amid the dominant necessity of sense, and on the other hand, the thought-content of consciousness (so far as secondary thoughts are concerned) is not wholly constituted by the selection of will.

Thus, on the whole there is a large primary region of secondary thought, as well as of the primary thoughts of sense-presentation, which is given in type. That is the way in which we do think of things, not wholly from any abstract necessity, so far as we know, but because we have inherited the method from an environment. It is the way we find ourselves thinking, a way which can only be fundamentally laid aside by an immense effort, and then only for isolated short periods of time. This is what I have called the "whole apparatus of commonsense thought."

It is this body of thought which is assumed in science. It is a way of thinking rather than a set of axioms. It is, in fact, the set of concepts which commonsense has found useful in sorting out human experience. It is modified in detail, but assumed in gross. The explanations of science are directed to finding conceptions and propositions concerning nature which explain the importance of these commonsense notions. For example, a chair is a commonsense notion, molecules and electrons explain our vision of chairs.

Now science aims at harmonising our reflective and derivative thoughts with the primary thoughts involved in the immediate apprehension of sense-presentation. It also aims at producing such derivative thoughts, logically knit together. This is scientific theory; and the harmony to be achieved is the agreement of theory with observation, which is the apprehension of sense-presentation.

Thus there is a two-fold scientific aim: (1) the production of theory which agrees with experience; and (2) the explanation of commonsense concepts of nature, at least in their main outlines. This explanation consists in the preservation of the concepts in a scientific theory of harmonised thought.

It is not asserted that this is what scientists in the past meant to achieve, or thought that they could achieve. It is suggested as the actual result of scientific effort, so far as that effort has had any measure of success. In short, we are here discussing the natural history of ideas and not volitions of scientists.

II. Objects

We perceive things in space. For example, among such things are dogs, chairs, curtains, drops of water, gusts of air, flames, rainbows, chimes of bells, odours, aches and pains. There is a scientific explanation of the origin of these perceptions. This explanation is given in terms of molecules, atoms, electrons, and their mutual relations, in particular of their space-relations, and waves of disturbance of these space-relations which are propagated through space. The primary elements of the scientific explanation— molecules, etc.—are not the things directly perceived. For example, we do not perceive a wave of light; the sensation of sight is the resultant effect of the impact of millions of such waves through a stretch of time. Thus the object directly perceived corresponds to a series of events in the physical world, events which are prolonged through a stretch of time. Nor is it true that a perceived object always corresponds to the same group of molecules. After a few years we recognise the same cat, but we are thereby related to different molecules.

Again, neglecting for a moment the scientific explanation, the perceived object is largely the supposition of our imagination. When we recognised the cat, we also recognised that it was glad to see us. But we merely heard its mewing, saw it arch its back, and felt it rubbing itself against us. We must distinguish, therefore, between the many direct objects of sense, and the single indirect object of thought which is the cat.

Thus, when we say that we perceived the cat and understood its feelings, we mean that we heard a sense-object of sound, that we saw a sense-object of sight, that we felt a sense-object of touch, and that we thought of a cat and imagined its feelings.

Sense-objects are correlated by time-relations and space-relations. Those simultaneous sense-objects which are also spatially coincident, are combined by thought into the perception of one cat. Such combination of sense-objects is an instinctive immediate judgment in general without effort of reasoning. Sometimes only one sense-object is present. For example, we hear mewing and say there must be a cat in the room. The transition from the sense-object to the cat has then been made, by deliberate ratiocinations. Even the concurrence of sense-objects may provoke such a self-conscious effort. For example, in the dark we feel something, and hear mewing from the same place, and think, Surely this is a cat. Sight is more bold; when we see a cat, we do not think further. We identify the sight with the cat, whereas the cat and the mew are separate. But such immediate identification of a sight-object and an object of thought may lead to error; the birds pecked at the grapes of Apelles.

A single sense-object is a complex entity. The sight-object of a tile on the hearth may remain unchanged as we watch it in a steady light, remaining ourselves unchanged in position. Even then it is prolonged in time, and has parts in space. Also it is somewhat arbitrarily distinguished from a larger whole of which it forms part. But the glancing firelight and a change in our position alters the sight-object. We judge that the tile thought-object remains unchanged. The sight-object of the coal on the fire gradually modifies, though within short intervals it remains unchanged. We judge that the coal thought-object is changing. The flame is never the same, and its shape is only vaguely distinguishable.

We conclude that a single self-identical sight-object is already a phantasy of thought. Consider the unchanging sight-object of the tile, as we remain still in a steady light. Now a sense-object perceived at one time is a distinct object from a sense-object seen at another time. Thus the sight of the tile at noon is distinct from its sight at 12.30. But there is no such thing as a sense-object at an instant. As we stare at the tile, a minute, or a second, or a tenth of a second, has flown by: essentially there is a duration. There is a stream of sight, and we can distinguish its parts. But the parts also are streams, and it is only in thought that the stream separates into a succession of elements. The stream may be "steady" as in the case of the unchanging sight-tile, or may be "turbulent" as in the case of the glancing sight-flame. In either case a sight-object is some arbitrarily small part of the stream.

Again, the stream which forms the succession of sight-tiles is merely a distinguishable part of the whole stream of sight-presentation.

So, finally, we conceive ourselves each experiencing a complete time-flux (or stream) of sense-presentation. This stream is distinguishable into parts. The grounds of distinction are differences of sense—including within that term, differences of types of sense, and differences of quality and of intensity within the same type of sense—and differences of time-relations, and differences of space-relations. Also the parts are not mutually exclusive and exist in unbounded variety.

The time-relation between the parts raises the questions of memory and recognition, subjects too complex for discussion here. One remark must be made. If it be admitted, as stated above, that we live in durations and not in instants, namely, that the present essentially occupies a stretch of time, the distinction between memory and immediate presentation cannot be quite fundamental; for always we have with us the fading present as it becomes the immediate past. This region of our consciousness is neither pure memory nor pure immediate presentation. Anyhow, memory is also a presentation in consciousness.

Another point is to be noted in connection with memory. There is no directly perceived time-relation between a present event and a past event. The present event is only related to the memory of the past event. But the memory of a past event is itself a present element in consciousness. We assert the principle that directly comparable relations can only exist between elements of consciousness, both in that present during which the perception occurs. All other relations between elements of perception are inferential constructions. It thus becomes necessary to explain how discriminations in the stream of events establish themselves and how the apparent world fails to collapse into one single present. The solution of the difficulty is arrived at by observing that the present is itself a duration, and therefore includes directly perceived time-relations between events contained within it. In other words we put the present on the same footing as the past and the future in respect to the inclusion within it of antecedent and succeeding events, so that past, present, and future are in this respect exactly analogous ideas. Thus there will be two events a and b, both in the same present, but the event a

will be directly perceived to precede the event *b*. Again time flows on, and the event *a* fades into the past, and in the new present duration events *b* and *c* occur, event *b* preceding event *c*, also in the same present duration there is the memory of the time-relation between *a* and *b*. Then by an inferential construction the event *a* in the past precedes the event *c* in the present. By proceeding according to this principle the time-relations between elements of consciousness, not in the same present, are established. The method of procedure here explained is a first example of what we will call the Principle of Aggregation. This is one of the fundamental principles of mental construction according to which our conception of the external physical world is constructed. Other examples will later on be met with.

The space-relations between the parts are confused and fluctuating, and in general lack determinate precision. The master-key by which we confine our attention to such parts as possess mutual relations sufficiently simple for our intellects to consider is the principle of convergence to simplicity with diminution of extent. We will call it the "principle of convergence." This principle extends throughout the whole field of sense-presentation.

The first application of the principle occurs in respect to time. The shorter the stretch of time, the simpler are the aspects of the sense-presentation contained within it. The perplexing effects of change are diminished and in many cases can be neglected. Nature has restricted the acts of thought which endeavour to realise the content of the present, to stretches of time sufficiently short to secure this static simplicity over the greater part of the sense-stream.

Spatial relations become simplified within the approximately static sense-world of the short time. A further simplicity is gained by partitioning this static world into parts of restricted space-content. The various parts thus obtained have simpler mutual space-relations, and again the principle of convergence holds.

Finally, the last simplicity is obtained by partitioning the parts, already restricted as to space and time, into further parts characterised by homogeneity in type of sense, and homogeneity in quality and intensity of sense. These three processes of restriction yield, finally, the sense-objects which have been mentioned above. Thus the sense-object is the result of an active process of discrimination made in virtue of the principle of convergence. It is the result of the quest for simplicity of relations within the complete stream of sense-presentation.

The thought-objects of perception are instances of a fundamental law of nature, the law of objective stability. It is the law of coherence of sense-objects. This law of stability has an application to time and an application to space; also it must be applied in conjunction with that other law, the principle of convergence to simplicity from which sense-objects are derived.

Some composite partial streams of sense-presentation can be distinguished with the following characteristics: (1) the time-succession of sense-objects, belonging to a single sense, involved in any such a composite partial stream, is composed of very similar objects whose modifications increase only gradually, and thus forms a homogeneous component stream within the composite stream; (2) the space-relations of those sense-objects (of various senses) of such a composite stream which are confined within any sufficiently short time are identical so far as they are definitely apprehended, and thus these various component streams, each homogeneous, "cohere" to form the whole composite partial stream; (3) there are other sense-presentations occurring in association with that composite partial stream which can be determined by rules derived from analogous composite partial streams, with other space and time relations, provided that the analogy be sufficiently close. Call these the "associated sense-presentations." A partial stream of this sort, viewed as a whole, is here called a "first crude thought-object of perception."

For example, we look at an orange for half a minute, handle it, and smell it, note its position in the fruit-basket, and then turn away. The stream of sense-presentation of the orange during that half-minute is a first crude thought-object of perception. Among the associated sense presentations are those of the fruit-basket which we conceive as supporting the orange.

The essential ground of the association of sense-objects of various types, perceived within one short duration, into a first crude thought-object of perception is the coincidence of their space-relations, that is, in general an approximate coincidence of such relations perhaps only vaguely apprehended. Thus coincident space-relations associate sense-objects into a first crude thought-object, and diverse space-relations dissociate sense-objects from aggregation into a first crude thought-object. In respect to some groups of sense-objects the association may be an immediate judgment devoid of all inference, so that the primary perceptual thought is that of the first crude thought-object, and the separate sense-objects are the result of reflective analysis acting on memory. For example sense-objects of sight and sense-objects of touch are often thus primarily associated and only secondarily dissociated in thought. But sometimes the association is wavering and indeterminate, for example, that between the sound-object of the mew of the cat and the sight-object of the cat. Thus to sum up, the partial stream of sense-perceptions coalesces into that first crude thought-object of perception which is the momentary cat because the sense-perceptions belonging to this stream are in the same place, but equally it would be true to say that they are in the same place because they belong to the same momentary cat. This analysis of the complete stream of sense-presentation in any small present duration into a variety of first crude thought-objects only partially fits the facts; for one reason because many sense-objects, such as sound for instance, have vague and indeterminate space-relations, for example vaguely those space-relations which we associate with our organs of sense and also vaguely those of the origin from which (in the scientific explanation) they proceed.

The procedure by which the orange of half a minute is elaborated into the orange in the ordinary sense of the term involves in addition the two principles of aggregation and of hypothetical sense-presentation.

The principle of aggregation, as here employed, takes the form that many distinct first crude thought-objects of perception, are conceived as one thought-object of perception, if the many partial streams forming these objects are sufficiently analogous, if their times of occurrence are distinct, and if the associated sense-presentations are sufficiently analogous.

For example, after leaving the orange, in five minutes we return. A new first crude thought-object of perception presents itself to us, indistinguishable from the half-minute orange we previously experienced; it is in the same fruit-basket. We aggregate the two presentations of an orange into the same orange. By such aggregations we obtain "second crude thought-objects of perception." But however far we can proceed with aggregation of this type, the orange is more than that. For example, what do we mean when we say, The orange is in the cupboard, if Tom has not eaten it?

The world of present fact is more than a stream of sense-presentation. We find ourselves with emotions, volitions, imaginations, conceptions, and judgments. No factor which enters into consciousness is by itself or even can exist in isolation. We are analysing certain relations between sense-presentation and other factors of consciousness. Hitherto we have taken into account merely the factors of concept and judgment. Imagination is necessary to complete the orange, namely, the imagination of hypothetical sense-presentations. It is beside the point to argue whether we ought to have such imaginations, or to discuss what are the metaphysical truths concerning reality to which they correspond. We are here only concerned with the fact that such imaginations exist and essentially enter into the formation of the concepts of the thought-objects of perception which are the first data of science. We conceive the orange as a permanent collection of sense-presentations existing as if they were an actual element in our consciousness, which they are not. The orange is thus conceived as in the cupboard with its shape, odour, colour, and other qualities. Namely, we imagine hypothetical possibilities of sense-presentation, and conceive their want of actuality in our consciousness as immaterial to their existence in fact. The fact which is essential for science is our conception; its meaning in regard to the metaphysics of reality is of no scientific importance, so far as physical science is concerned.

The orange completed in this way is the thought-object of perception.

It must be remembered that the judgments and concepts arising in the formation of thought-objects of perception are in the main instinctive judgments, and instinctive concepts, and are not concepts and judgments consciously sought for and consciously criticised before adoption. Their adoption is facilitated by and interwoven with the expectation of the future in which the hypothetical passes into the actual, and also with the further judgment of the existence of other consciousnesses; so that much that is hypothetical to one consciousness is judged to be actual to others.

The thought-object of perception is, in fact, a device to make plain to our reflective consciousness relations which hold within the complete stream of sense-presentation. Concerning the utility of this weapon there can be no question; it is the rock upon which the whole structure of commonsense thought is erected. But when we consider the limits of its application the evidence is confused. A great part of our sense-presentation can be construed as perception of various persistent thought-objects. But hardly at any time can the sense-presentations be construed wholly in that way. Sights lend themselves easily to this construction, but sight can be baffled: for example, consider reflections in looking-glasses, apparently bent sticks half in and half out of water, rainbows, brilliant patches of light which conceal the object from which they emanate, and many analogous phenomena. Sound is more difficult; it tends largely to disengage itself from any such object. For example, we see the bell, but we hear the sound which comes from the bell; yet we also say that we hear the bell. Again, a toothache is largely by itself, and is only indirectly a perception of the nerve of the tooth. Illustrations to the same effect can be accumulated from every type of sensation.

Another difficulty arises from the fact of change. The thought-object is conceived as one thing, wholly actual at each instant. But since the meat has been bought it has been cooked, the grass grows and then withers, the coal burns in the fire, the pyramids of Egypt remain unchanged for ages, but even the pyramids are not wholly unchanged. The difficulty of change is merely evaded by affixing a technical Latin name to a supposed logical fallacy. A slight cooking leaves the meat the same object, but two days in the oven burns it to a cinder. When does the meat cease to be? Now the chief use of the thought-object is the concept of it as one thing, here and now, which later can be recognised, there and then. This concept applies sufficiently well to most things for short times, and to many things for long times. But sense-presentation as a whole entirely refuses to be patient of the concept.

We have now come to the reflective region of explanation, which is science.

A great part of the difficulty is at once removed by applying the principle of convergence to simplicity. We habitually make our thought-objects too large; we should think in smaller parts. For example, the Sphinx has changed by its nose becoming chipped, but by proper inquiry we could find the missing part in some private house of Western Europe or Northern America. Thus, either part, the rest of the Sphinx or the chip, regains its permanence. Furthermore, we enlarge this explanation by conceiving parts so small that they can only be observed under the most favourable circumstances. This is a wide extension of the principle of convergence in its application to nature; but it is a principle amply supported by the history of exact observation.

Thus, change in thought-objects of perception is largely explained as a disintegration into smaller parts, themselves thought-objects of perception. The thought-objects of perception which are presupposed in the common thought of civilised beings are almost wholly hypothetical. The material universe is largely a concept of the imagination which rests on a slender basis of direct sense-presentation. But none the less it is a fact; for it is a fact that actually we imagine it. Thus it is actual in our consciousness just as sense-presentation also is actual there. The effort of reflective criticism is to make these two factors in our consciousness agree where they are related, namely, to construe our sense-presentation as actual realisation of the hypothetical thought-objects of perception.

The wholesale employment of purely hypothetical thought-objects of perception enables science to explain some of the stray sense-objects which cannot be construed as perceptions of a thought-object of perception: for example, sounds. But the phenomena as a whole defy explanation on these lines until a further fundamental step is taken, which transforms the whole concept of the material universe. Namely, the thought-object of perception is superseded by the thought-object of science.

The thought-objects of science are molecules, atoms, and electrons. The peculiarity of these objects is that they have shed all the qualities which are capable of direct sense-representation in consciousness. They are known to us only by their associated phenomena, namely, series of events in which they are implicated are represented in our consciousness by sense-presentations. In this way, the thought-objects of science are conceived as the causes of sense-representation. The transition from thought-objects of perception to thought-objects of science is decently veiled by an elaborate theory concerning primary and secondary qualities of bodies.

This device, by which sense-presentations are represented in thought as our perception of events in which thought-objects of science are implicated, is the fundamental means by which a bridge is formed between the fluid vagueness of sense and the exact definition of thought. In thought a proposition is either true or false, an entity is exactly what it is, and relations between entities are expressible (in idea) by definite propositions about distinctly conceived entities. Sense-perception knows none of these things, except by courtesy. Accuracy essentially collapses at some stage of inquiry.

III. Time and Space

Recapitulation.—Relations of time and relations of space hold between sense-objects of perception. These sense-objects are distinguished as separate objects by the recognition of either (1) differences of sense-content, or (2) time-relations between them other than simultaneity, or (3) space-relations between them other than coincidence. Thus sense-objects arise from the recognition of contrast within the complete stream of sense-presentation, namely, from the recognition of the objects as related terms, by relations which contrast them. Differences of sense-content are infinitely complex in their variety. Their analysis under the heading of general ideas is the unending task of physical science. Time-relations and space-relations are comparatively simple, and the general ideas according to which their analysis should proceed are obvious.

This simplicity of time and space is perhaps the reason why thought chooses them as the permanent ground for objectival distinction, throwing the various sense-objects thus obtainable into one heap, as a first crude thought-object of perception, and thence, as described above, obtaining a thought-object of perception. Thus a thought-object of perception conceived as in the present of a short duration is a first crude thought-object of perception either actual or hypothetical. Such a thought-object of perception, confined within a short duration, takes on the space-relations of its component sense-objects within that same duration. Accordingly thought-objects of perception, conceived in their whole extents, have to each other the time-relationships of their complete existences, and within any small duration have to each other the space-relationships of their component sense-objects which lie within that duration.

Relations bind together: thus thought-objects of perception are connected in time and in space. The genesis of the objectival analysis of sense-presentation is the recognition of sense-objects as distinct terms in time-relations and space-relations: thus thought-objects of perception are separated by time and by space.

Whole and Part.—A sense-object is part of the complete stream of presentation. This concept of being a part is merely the statement of the relation of the sense-object to the complete sense-presentation for that consciousness. Also a sense-object can be part of another sense-object. It can be a part in two ways, namely, a part in time and a part in space. It seems probable that both these concepts of time-part and space-part are fundamental; that is, are concepts expressing relations which are directly presented to us, and are not concepts about concepts. In that case no further definition of the actual presentation is possible. It may even then be possible to define an adequate criterion of the occurrence of such a presentation. For example, adopting for the moment a realist metaphysic as to the existence of the physical world of molecules and electrons, the vision of a chair as occurring for some definite person at some definite time is essentially indefinable. It is his vision, though each of us guesses that it must be uncommonly like our vision under analogous circumstances. But the existence of the definable molecules and waves of light in certain definable relations to his bodily organs of sense, his body also being in a certain definable state, forms an adequate criterion of the occurrence of the vision, a criterion which is accepted in Courts of Law and which physical science tacitly substitutes for the vision.

The connection between the relations "whole and part" and "all and some" is intimate. It can be explained thus so far as concerns directly presented sense-objects. Call two sense-objects "separated" if there is no third sense-object which is a part of both of them. Then an object A is composed of the two objects B and C, if (1) B and C, are both parts of A, (2) B and C are separated, and (3) there is no part of A which is separated both from B and from C. In such a case the class α which is composed of the two objects B and C is often substituted in thought for the sense-object A. But this process presupposes the fundamental relation "whole and part." Conversely the objects B and C may be actual sense-objects, but the sense-object A which corresponds to the class α may remain hypothetical. For example, the round world on which we live remains a conception corresponding to no single sense-object at any time presented in any human being's consciousness.

It is possible, however, that some mode of conceiving the whole-and-part relation between extended objects as the all-and-some relation of logical classes can be found. But in this case the extended objects as here conceived cannot be the true sense-objects which are present to consciousness. For as here conceived a part of a sense-object is another sense-object of the same type; and there-fore one sense-object cannot be a class of other sense-objects, just as a tea-spoon cannot be a class of other tea-spoons. The ordinary way in thought by which whole-and-part is reduced to all-and-some is by the device of points, namely, the part of an object occupies some of the points occupied by the whole object. If any one holds that in his consciousness the sense-presentation is a presentation of point-objects, and that an extended object is merely a class of such point-objects collected together in thought, then this ordinary method is completely satisfactory. We shall proceed on the assump-tion that this conception of directly perceived point-objects has no relation to the facts.

In the preceding chapter on "The Organisation of Thought," another mode is suggested. But this method would apply only to the thought-object of perception, and has no reference to the primary sense-objects here considered. Accordingly it must reckon as a subordinate device for a later stage of thought.

Thus the point-object in time and the point-object in space, and the double point-object both in time and space, must be conceived as intellectual constructions. The fundamental fact is the sense-object, extended both in time and space, with the fundamental relation of whole-to-part to other such objects, and subject to the law of convergence to simplicity as we proceed in thought through a series of successively-contained parts.

The relation whole-to-part is a temporal or spacial relation, and is therefore primarily a relation holding between sense-objects of perception, and it is only derivatively ascribed to the thought-objects of perception of which they are components. More generally, space and time relations hold primarily between sense-objects of perception and derivatively between thought-objects of perception.

Definition of Points.—The genesis of points of time and of space can now be studied. We must distinguish (1) sense-time and sense-space, and (2) thought-time of perception and thought-space of perception.

Sense-time and sense-space are the actually observed time-relations and space-relations between sense-objects. Sense-time and sense-space have no points except, perhaps, a few sparse instances, sufficient to suggest the logical idea; also sense-time and sense-space are discontinuous and fragmentary.

Thought-time of perception and thought-space of perception are the time and space relations which hold between thought-objects of perception. Thought-time of perception and thought-space of perception are each continuous. By "continuous" is here meant that all thought-objects of perception have to each other a time (or space) relation.

The origin of points is the effort to take full advantage of the principle of convergence to simplicity. In so far as this principle does not apply, a point is merely a cumbrous way of directing attention to a set of relations between a certain set of thought-objects of perception, which set of relations, though actual so far as a thought-object is actual, is (under this supposition) of no particular importance. Thus the proved importance in physical science of the concepts of points in time and points in space is a tribute to the wide applicability of this principle of convergence.

Euclid defines a point as without parts and without magnitude. In modern language a point is often described as an ideal limit by indefinitely continuing the process of diminishing a volume (or area). Points as thus conceived are often called convenient fictions. This language is ambiguous. What is meant by a fiction? If it means a conception which does not correspond to any fact, there is some difficulty in understanding how it can be of any use in physical science. For example, the fiction of a red man in a green coat inhabiting the moon can never be of the slightest scientific service, simply because—as we may presume—it corresponds to no fact. By calling the concept of points a convenient fiction, it must be meant that the concept does correspond to some important facts. It is, then, requisite, in the place of such vague allusiveness, to explain exactly what are the facts to which the concept corresponds.

We are not much helped by explaining that a point is an ideal limit. What is a limit? The idea of a limit has a precise meaning in the theory of series, and in the theory of the values of functions; but neither of these meanings apply here. It may be observed that, before the ordinary mathematical meanings of limit had received a precise explanation, the idea of a point as a limit might be considered as one among other examples of an idea only to be apprehended by direct intuition. This view is not now open to us. Thus, again, we are confronted with the question: What are the precise properties meant when a point is described as an ideal limit? The discussion which now follows is an attempt to express the concept of a point in terms of thought-objects of perception related together by the whole-and-part relation, considered either as a time-relation or as a space-relation. If it is so preferred, it may be considered that the discussion is directed towards a precise elucidation of the term "ideal limit" as often used in this connection.

The subsequent explanations can be made easier to follow by a small piece of symbolism: Let aEb mean that *"b is part of a."* We need not decide whether we are talking of time-parts or space-parts, but whichever choice is supposed to be made must be conceived as adhered to throughout any connected discussion. The symbol E may be considered as the initial letter of "encloses," so we read *"aEb"* as *"a encloses b."* Again the "field of E" is the set of things which either enclose or are enclosed, *i.e.* everything *"a,"* which is such that x can be found so that either aEx or xEa. A member of the field of E is called "an enclosure-object."

Now, we assume that this relation of whole-to-part, which in the future we will call "enclosure," always satisfies the conditions in that the relation E is (1) transitive, (2) asymmetrical, and (3) with its domain including its converse domain.

These four conditions deserve some slight consideration; only the first two of them embody hypotheses which enter vitally into the reasoning.

Condition (1) may be stated as the condition that aEb and bEc always implies aEc. The fact that an entity b can be found such that aEb and bEc may be conceived as a relation between a and c. It is natural to write E^2 for this relation. Thus the condition is now written: If aE^2c, then aEc. This can be still otherwise expressed by saying that the relation E^2 implies, whenever it holds, that the relation E also holds.

Condition (2) is partly a mere question of trivial definition, and partly a substantial assumption. The asymmetrical relation (E) is such that aEb and bEa can never hold simultaneously. This property splits up into two parts: (1) that no instance of aEb and bEa and "a diverse from b," can occur, and (2) that aEa cannot occur. The first part is a substantial assumption, the second part (so far as we are concerned) reduces to the trivial convention that we shall not consider an object as part of itself, but will confine attention to "proper parts."

Condition (3) means that aEb always implies that c can be found such that bEc. This condition, taken in conjunction with the fact that we are only considering proper parts, is the assertion of the principle of the indefinite divisibility of extended objects, both in space and in time.

An indivisible part will lack duration in time, and extension in space, and is thus an entity of essentially a different character to a divisible part. If we admit such indivisibles as the only true sense-objects, our subsequent procedure is an unnecessary elaboration.

It will be found that a fourth condition is necessary owing to logical difficulties connected with the theory of an infinite number of choices. It will not be necessary for us to enter further on this question, which involves difficult considerations of abstract logic. The outcome is, that apart from hypothesis we cannot prove the existence of the sets, each containing an infinite number of objects, which are here called points, as will be explained immediately.

Now consider a set of enclosure objects which is such that (1) of any two of its members one encloses the other, and (2) there is no member which is enclosed by all the others, and (3) there is no enclosure-object, not a member of the set which is enclosed by every member of the set. Call such a set a "convergent set of enclosure-objects." As we pass along the series from larger to smaller members, evidently we converge towards an ideal simplicity to any degree of approximation to which we like to proceed, and the series as a whole embodies the complete ideal along that route of approximation. In fact, to repeat, the series is a *route of approximation.*

We have now to inquire if the principle of convergence to simplicity may be expected to yield the same type of simplicity for every such convergent route. The answer is, as we might expect, namely, that this depends upon the nature of the properties which are to be simplified.

For example, consider the application to time. Now, time is one-dimensional; so when this property of one-dimensionality has been expressed by the proper conditions, not here stated, a convergent set of enclosure-objects must, considered as a route of approximation, exhibit the properties of one unique instant of time, as ordinarily conceived by the Euclidean definition. Accordingly, whatever simplicity is to be achieved by the application to time of the principle of convergence to simplicity must be exhibited among the properties of any such route of approximation.

For space, different considerations arise. Owing to its multiple dimensions, we can show that different convergent sets of enclosure-objects, indicating different routes of approximation, may exhibit convergence to different types of simplicity, some more complex than others.

For example, consider a rectangular box of height h ft., breadth b ft., and thickness c ft. Now, keep h and b constant, and let the central plane (height h, breadth b) perpendicular to the thickness be fixed, then make c diminish indefinitely. We thus obtain a convergent series of an indefinitely large number of boxes, and there is no smallest box. Thus this convergent series exhibits the route of approximation towards the type of simplicity expressed as being a plane area of height h, breadth b, and no thickness.

Again, by keeping the central line of height h fixed, and by making b and c diminish indefinitely, the series converges to the segment of a straight line of length h.

Finally, by keeping only the central point fixed, and by making h, b, and c diminish indefinitely, the series converges to a point.

Furthermore, we have introduced as yet no concept which would prevent an enclosure-object being formed of detached fragments in space. Thus we can easily imagine a convergent set which converges to a number of points in space. For example, each object of the set might be formed of two not overlapping spheres of radius r, with centres A and B. Then by diminishing r indefinitely, and keeping A and B fixed, we have convergence to the pair of points A and B.

It remains now to consider how those convergent sets which converge to a single point can be discriminated from all the other types of such sets, merely by utilising concepts founded on the relation of enclosure.

Let us name convergent sets by Greek letters; by proceeding "forward" along any such set let us understand the process of continually passing from the larger to the smaller enclosure-objects which form the set.

The convergent set α will be said to "cover" the convergent set β, if every member of α encloses some members of β. We notice that if an enclosure-object x encloses any member (y) of β, then every member of the "tail-end" of β, found by proceeding forward along β from y, must be enclosed by x. Thus if α covers β, every member of α encloses every member of the tail-end of β, starting from the largest member of β which is enclosed by that member of α.

It is possible for each of two convergent sets to cover the other. For example, let one set (α) be a set of concentric spheres converging to their centre A, and the other set (β) be a set of concentric cubes, similarly situated, converging to the same centre A. Then α and β will each cover the other.

Let two convergent sets which are such that each covers the other be called "equal."

Then it is a sufficient condition to secure that a convergent set α possesses the point type of convergence, if every convergent set covered by it is also equal to it, namely, α is a convergent set with the punctual type of convergence, if "α covers β" always implies that β covers α.

It can easily be seen by simple examples that the other types of convergence to surfaces or lines or sets of points cannot possess this property. Consider, for example, the three convergent sets of boxes in the preceding illustration, which converge respectively to a central plane, a central line in the central plane, and the central point in the central line. The first set covers the second and third sets, and the second set covers the third set, but no two of the sets are equal.

It is a more difficult question to determine whether the condition here indicated as sufficient to secure the punctual type of convergence is also necessary. The question turns on how far thought-objects of perception possess exact boundaries prior to the elaboration of exact mathematical concepts of space. If they are to be conceived as possessing such exact boundaries, then convergent sets converging to points on such boundaries must be allowed for. The procedure necessary for the specification of the complete punctual condition becomes then very elaborate,[1] and will not be considered here.

But such exact determination as is involved in the conception of an exact spatial boundary does not seem to belong to the true thought-object of perception. The ascription of an exact boundary really belongs to the transition stage of thought as it passes from the thought-object of perception to the thought-object of science. The transition from the sense-object immediately presented to the thought-object of perception is historically made in a wavering indeterminate line of thought. The definite stages here marked out simply serve to prove that a logically explicable transition is possible.

We accordingly assume that the condition laid down above to secure the punctual convergence of a convergent set of enclosure-objects is not only sufficient, but necessary.

It can be proved that, if two convergent sets of enclosure-objects are both equal to a third convergent set, they are equal to each other. Consider now any punctual convergent set (α). We want to define the "point" to which α is a route of approximation in a way which is neutral between α and all the convergent sets which are equal to α. Each of these sets is a route of approximation to the same

---

[1] Cf. *Révue de Métaphysique et de Morale*, May 1916, where this question is dealt with by the author at the end of an article, "La théorie relationniste de l'espace." [Addendum, 1928: The article was written in 1914, and read in Paris at a congress in May of that year. I do not now consider that it evades the difficulty. The topic is reconsidered in my Gifford lectures for 1928.]

"point" as α. This definition is secured if we define the point as the class formed by all the enclosure-objects which belong either to α or to any convergent set which is equal to α. Let P be this class of enclosure-objects. Then any convergent set (β) which consists of enclosure-objects entirely selected from members of the class P must be a route of approximation to the same "point" as does the original punctual set α; namely, provided that we choose a small enough enclosure-object in β, we can always find a member of α which encloses it; and provided that we choose a small enough enclosure-object in α, we can always find a member of β which encloses it. Thus P only includes convergent sets of the punctual type, and the route of approximation indicated by any two convergent sets selected from P converges to identical results.

The Uses of Points.—The sole use of points is to facilitate the employment of the principle of Convergence to Simplicity. By this principle some simple relations in appropriate circumstances become true, when objects are considered which are sufficiently restricted in time or in space. The introduction of points enables this principle to be carried through to its ideal limit. For example, suppose $g(a, b, c)$ represents some statement concerning three enclosure-objects, a, b, c, which may be true if the objects are sufficiently restricted in extent. Let A, B, C be three given points, then we define $g(A, B, C)$ to mean that *whatever* three enclosure-objects a, b, c are chosen, such that a is a member of A, b of B, and c of C, it is *always possible* to find three other members of A, B, C, namely, x a member of A, y of B, and z of C, such that aEx, bEy, cEz, and $g(x, y, z)$. So by going far enough down in the tail-ends of A, B, C we can always secure three objects x, y, z for which $g(x, y, z)$ is true.

For example, let $g(A, B, C)$ mean "A, B, C are three points in a linear row." This must be construed to mean that whatever three objects a, b, c we choose, members of A, B, C respectively, we can always find three objects x, y, z, also members of A, B, C respectively, and such that a encloses x, b encloses y, c encloses z, and also such that x, y, z are in a linear row.

Sometimes a double convergence is necessary, namely, a convergence of conditions as well as a convergence of objects. For example, consider the statement, "the points A and B are two feet apart." Now, the exact statement "two feet apart" does not apply to objects. For objects x and y we must substitute the statement, "the distance between x and y lies between the limits $(2 \pm e)$ feet." Here e is some number, less than two, which w have chosen for this statement. Then the points A and B are two feet apart; if, *however we choose the number e*, whatever enclosure-objects a and b, members of A and B respectively, we consider, we can always find enclosure-objects x and y, members of A and B respectively, such that a encloses x and b encloses y, and also such that the distance between x and y lies between the limits $(2 \pm e)$ feet. It is evident, since e can be chosen as small as we please, that this statement exactly expresses the condition that A and B are two feet apart.

Straight Lines and Planes.—But the problem of the intellectual construction of straight lines and planes is not yet sufficiently analysed. We have interpreted the meaning of the statement that three or more points are collinear, and can similarly see how to interpret the meaning of the statement that four or more points are coplanar, in either case deriving the exact geometrical statements from vaguer statements respecting extended objects.

This procedure only contemplates groups of finite numbers of points. But straight lines and planes are conceived as containing infinite numbers of points. This completion of lines and planes is obtained by a renewed application of the principle of aggregation, just as a set of first crude thought-objects of perception are aggregated into one complete thought-object of perception. In this way repeated judgments of the collinearity of sets of points are finally, when certain conditions of interlacing are fulfilled, aggregated in the single judgment of all the points of the groups as forming one whole collinear group. Similarly for judgments of coplanarity. This process of logical aggregation can be exhibited in its exact logical analysis. But it is unnecessary here to proceed to such details. Thus we conceive our points as sorted into planes and straight lines, concerning which the various axioms of geometry hold. These axioms, in so far as they essentially require the conception of points, are capable of being exhibited as the outcome of vaguer, less exact judgments respecting the relations of extended objects.

Empty Space.—It must be observed that the points, hitherto defined, necessarily involve thought-objects of perception, and lie within the space-extension occupied by such objects. It is true that such objects are largely hypothetical, and that we can bring into our hypotheses sufficient objects to complete our lines and planes. But every such hypothesis weakens the connection between our scientific concept of nature and the actual observed facts which are involved in the actual sense-presentations.

Occam's razor, *Entia non multiplicanda præter necessitatem*, is not an arbitrary rule based on mere logical elegancy. Nor is its application purely confined to metaphysical speculation. I am ignorant of the precise reason for its metaphysical validity, but its scientific validity is obvious, namely, every use of hypothetical entities diminishes the claim of scientific reasoning to be the necessary outcome of a harmony between thought and sense-presentation. As hypothesis increases, necessity diminishes.

Commonsense thought also supports this refusal to conceive of all space as essentially depending on hypothetical objects which fill it. We think of material objects as filling space, but we ask whether any objects exist between the Earth and the Sun, between the stars, or beyond the stars. For us, space is there; the only question is whether or not it be full. But this form of question presupposes the meaning of empty space, namely, of space not containing hypothetical objects.

This brings up a wider use of the concept of points, necessitating a wider definition. Hitherto we have conceived points as indicating relations of enclosure between objects. We thus arrive at what now we will term "material points." But the idea of points can now be transformed so as to indicate the possibilities of external relations not those of enclosure. This is effected by an enlargement of the concept of ideal points, already known to geometers.

Define "material lines" to be complete collinear classes of collinear points. Consider now the set of material lines which contain a certain material point. Call such a set of lines an ideal point. This set of lines indicates a possibility of position, which is in fact occupied by that material point common to all the material lines. So this ideal point is an occupied ideal point. Now consider a set of three material lines, such that any two are coplanar, but not the whole three, and further consider the complete set of material lines such that each is coplanar with each of the three material lines first chosen. The axioms which hold for the material lines will enable us to prove that any two lines of this set are coplanar. Then the whole set of lines, including the three original lines, forms an ideal point, according to the definition in its full generality. Such an ideal point may be occupied. In that case there is a material point common to all the lines of the set, but it may be unoccupied. Then the ideal point merely indicates a possibility of spatial relations which has not been realised. It is the point of empty space. Thus the ideal points, which may or may not be occupied, are the points of geometry viewed as an applied science. These points are distributed into straight lines and planes. But any further discussion of this question will lead us into the technical subject of the axioms of geometry and their immediate consequences. Enough has been said to show how geometry arises according to the relational theory of space.

Space as thus conceived is the thought-space of the material world.

IV. Fields of Force

The thought-objects of science are conceived as directly related to this thought-space. Their spatial relations are among those indicated by the points of the thought-space. Their emergence in science has been merely a further development of processes already inherent in commonsense thought.

Relations within the complete sense-presentation were represented in thought by the concept of thought-objects of perception. All sense-presentation could not be represented in this way; also the change and disappearance of thought-objects occasioned confusion of thought. A reduction of this confusion to order was attempted by the concepts of permanent matter with primary and secondary qualities. Finally, this has issued in the secondary qualities being traced as perception of events generated by the objects, but—as perceived—entirely disconnected with them. Also the thought-objects of perception have been replaced by molecules and electrons and ether-waves, until at length it is never the thought-object of science which is perceived, but complicated series of events in which they are implicated. If science be right, nobody ever perceived a thing, but only an event. The result is, that the older language of philosophy which still survives in many quarters is now thoroughly confusing when brought into connection with the modern concepts of science. Philosophy—that is, the older philosophy—conceives the thing as directly perceived. According to scientific thought, the ultimate thing is never perceived, perception essentially issuing from a series of events. It is impossible to reconcile the two points of view.

The advantage of the modern scientific concept is that it is enabled to "explain" the fluid vague outlines of sense-presentation. The thought-object of perception is now conceived as a fairly stable state of motion of a huge group of molecules, constantly changing, but preserving a certain identity of characteristics. Also stray sense-objects, not immediately given as part of a thought-object of perception, are now explicable: the dancing light-reflection, the vaguely heard sound, the smell. In fact, the perceived events of the scientific world have the same general definition and lack of definition, and the same general stability and lack of stability, as the sense-objects of the complete sense-presentation or as the thought-objects of perception.

The thought-objects of science, namely, molecules, atoms, and electrons, have gained in permanence. The events are reduced to changes in space-configuration. The laws determining these changes are the ultimate laws of nature.

The laws of change in the physical universe proceed on the assumption that the preceding states of the universe determine the character of the change. Thus, to know the configurations and events of the universe up to and including any instant would involve sufficient data from which to determine the succession of events throughout all time.

But in tracing the antecedents of events, commonsense thought, dealing with the world of thought-objects of perception, habitually assumes that the greater number of antecedent events can be neglected as irrelevant. Consideration of causes is restricted to a few events during a short preceding interval. Finally, in scientific thought it has been assumed that the events in an arbitrarily small preceding duration are sufficient. Thus physical quantities and their successive differential co-efficients up to any order at the instant, but with their limiting values just before that instant, are on this theory sufficient to determine the state of the universe at all times after the instant. More particular laws are assumed. But the search for them is guided by this general principle. Also it is assumed that the greater number of events in the physical universe are irrelevant to the production of any particular effect, which is assumed to issue from relatively few antecedents. These assumptions have grown out of the experience of mankind. The first lesson of life is to concentrate attention on few factors of sense-presentations, and on still fewer of the universe of thought-objects of perception.

The principle by which—consciously or unconsciously—thought has been guided is that in searching for particular causes, remoteness in time and remoteness in space are evidences of comparative disconnection of influence. The extreme form of this principle is the denial of any action at a distance either in time or space. The difficulty in accepting this principle in its crude form is, that since there are no contiguous points, only coincident bodies can act on each other. I can see no answer to this difficulty—namely, either bodies have the same location and are thus coincident, or they have different locations and are thus at a distance and do not act on each other.

This difficulty is not evaded by the hypothesis of an ether, continuously distributed. For two reasons: in the first place, the continuity of the ether does not avoid the dilemma; and secondly, the difficulty applies to time as well as to space, and the dilemma would prove that causation producing change is impossible, namely, no changed condition could be the result of antecedent circumstances.

On the other hand, a direct interaction between two bodies separated in space undoubtedly offends the conception of distance as implying physical disconnection as well as spatial relation. There is no logical difficulty in the assumption of action at a distance as in the case of its denial, but it is contradictory to persistent assumptions of that apparatus of commonsense thought which it is the main business of science to harmonise with sense-presentation, employing only the minimum of modification.

Modern science is really unconcerned with this debate. Its (unacknowledged) conceptions are really quite different, though the verbal explanations retain the form of a previous epoch. The point of the change in conception is that the old thought-object of science was conceived as possessing a simplicity not belonging to the material universe as a whole. It was secluded within a finite region of space, and changes in its circumstances could only arise from forces which formed no essential part of its nature. An ether was called into existence to explain the active relations between these passive thought-objects. The whole conception suffers from the logical difficulties noted above. Also no clear conception can be formed of the sense in which the ether is explanatory. It is to possess a type of activity denied to the original thought-object, namely, it carries potential energy, whereas the atom possessed only kinetic energy, the so-called potential energy of an atom belonging really to the surrounding ether. The truth is, that ether is really excepted from the axiom "no action at a distance," and the axiom thereby is robbed of all its force.

The modern thought-object of science—not yet explicitly acknowledged—has the complexity of the whole material universe. In physics, as elsewhere, the hopeless endeavour to derive complexity from simplicity has been tacitly abandoned. What is aimed at is not simplicity, but persistence and regularity. In a sense regularity is a sort of simplicity. But it is the simplicity of stable mutual relations, and not the simplicity of absence of types of internal structure or of type of relation. This thought-object fills all space. It is a "field"; that is to say, it is a certain distribution of scalar and vector quantities throughout space, these quantities having each its value for each point of space at each point of time, being continuously distributed throughout space and throughout time, possibly with some exceptional discontinuities. The various types of quantity which form the field have fixed relations to each other at each point of time and space. These relations are the ultimate laws of nature.

For example, consider an electron. There is a scalar distribution of electricity, which is what is ordinarily called the electron. This scalar distribution has a volume-density ϱ at the time t at any point (x, y, z). Thus ϱ is a function of (x, y, z, t), which is zero except within a restricted region. Furthermore, at any time t, as an essential adjunct, there is a continuous space distribution at each point of the two vectors (X, Y, Z), which is the electric force, and (α, β, γ), which is the magnetic force. Lastly, individuality is ascribed to the scalar electric distribution, so that in addition to its conservation of quantity—involved in the assumed laws—it is also possible to assign the velocities with which the various individual parts of the distribution are moving. Let (u, v, w) be this velocity at (x, y, z, t).

This whole scheme of scalar and vector quantities, namely, ϱ, (X, Y, Z), (α, β, γ), (u, v, w) is interconnected by the electromagnetic laws. It follows from these laws that the electron, in the sense of the scalar distribution ϱ, is to be conceived as at each instant propagating from itself an emanation which travels outwards with the velocity of light *in vacuo,* and from which (X, Y, Z) and (α, β, γ) can be calculated, so far as they are due to that. Thus the field, at any time, due to the electron as a whole depends on the previous history of the electron, the nearer to the electron the more recent being the relevant history. The whole scheme of such a field is one single thought-object of science: the electron and its emanations form one essential whole, namely one thought-object of science, essentially complex and essentially filling all space. The electron proper, namely, the scalar distribution ϱ, is the focus of the whole, the essential focal property being that the field at any instant is completely determined by the previous history of the focus and of its space relations through all previous time. But the field and the focus are not independent concepts, they are essentially correlated in one organised unity, namely, they are essentially correlated terms in the field of one relation in virtue of which the entities enter into our thoughts.

The fields of a group of electrons are superposed according to the linear law for aggregation, namely, pure addition for analogous scalar quantities and the parallelogram law for analogous vectors. The changes in motion of each electron depend entirely on the resultant field in the region it occupies. Thus a field can be viewed as a possibility of action, but a possibility which represents an actuality.

It is to be noted that the two alternative views of causation are here both included. The complete field within any region of space depends on the past histories of all the electrons, histories extending backwards in proportion to their distances. Also this dependence can be conceived as a transmission. But viewing the cause which effects changes on the electron within that region, it is solely that field within the region, which field is coincident with that electron both in time and in space.

This process of conceiving the actuality underlying a possibility is the uniform process by which regularity and permanence is introduced into scientific thought, namely, we proceed from the actuality of the fact to the actuality of possibility.

In conformity with this principle, propositions are the outgrowth from actual thought-expressions, thought-objects of perceptions from crude sense-objects, hypothetical thought-objects of perception from actual thought-objects of perception, material points from hypothetical infinite suites of hypothetical thought-objects of perception, ideal points from material points, thought-objects of science from thought-objects of perception, fields of electrons from actual mutual reactions of actual electrons.

The process is a research for permanence, uniformity, and simplicity of logical relation. But it does not issue in simplicity of internal structure. Each ultimate thought-object of science retains every quality attributed to the whole scientific universe, but retains them in a form characterised by permanence and uniformity.

V. Conclusion

We commenced by excluding judgments of worth and ontological judgments. We conclude by recalling them. Judgments of worth are no part of the texture of physical science, but they are part of the motive of its production. Mankind have raised the edifice of science, because they have judged it worth while. In other words, the motives involve innumerable judgments of value. Again, there has been conscious selection of the parts of the scientific field to be cultivated, and this conscious selection involves judgments of value. These values may be æsthetic, or moral, or utilitarian, namely, judgments as to the beauty of the structure, or as to the duty of exploring the truth, or as to utility in the satisfaction of physical wants. But whatever the motive, without judgments of value there would have been no science.

Again, ontological judgments were not excluded by reason of any lack of interest. They are in fact presupposed in every act of life: in our affections, in our self-restraints, and in our constructive efforts.

They are presupposed in moral judgments. The difficulty about them is the absence of agreement as to the method of harmonising the crude judgments of commonsense.

Science does not diminish the need of a metaphysic. Where this need is most insistent is in connection with what above has been termed "the actuality underlying a possibility." A few words of explanation may render the argument clearer, although they involve a rash approach to metaphysical heights which it is not the purpose of this paper to explore.

The conception of subject and object in careless discussion covers two distinct relations. There is the relation of the whole perceiving consciousness to part of its own content, for example, the relation of a perceiving consciousness to an object of redness apparent to it. There is also the relation of a perceiving consciousness to an entity which does not exist in virtue of being part of the content of that consciousness. Such a relation, so far as known to the perceiving consciousness, must be an inferred relation, the inference being derived from an analysis of the content of the perceiving consciousness.

The bases for such inferences must be elements in consciousness directly known as transcending their immediate presentation in consciousness. Such elements are universal logical truths, moral and æsthetic truths, and truths embodied in hypothetical propositions. These are the immediate objects of perception which are other than the mere affections of the perceiving subject. They have the property of being parts of the immediate presentations for individual subjects and yet more than such parts. All other existence is inferred existence.

In this chapter we are more directly concerned with truths embodied in hypothetical propositions. Such truths must not be confused with any doubtfulness which attaches to our judgments of the future course of natural phenomena. A hypothetical proposition, like a categorical judgment, may or may not be doubtful. Also like a categorical judgment, it expresses a fact. This fact is two-fold: as a presentation in consciousness, it is just this hypothetical judgment; as expressing a categorical fact, it states a relation which lies beyond consciousness, holding between entities thereby inferred.

But this metaphysical analysis, short though it be, is probably wrong, and at the best will only command very partial assent. Certainly; and this admission brings out the very point which I wished to make. Physical science is based on elements of thought, such as judgments registering actual perceptions, and judgments registering hypothetical perceptions which under certain circumstances would be realised. These elements form the agreed content of the apparatus of commonsense thought. They require metaphysical analysis; but they are among the data from which metaphysics starts. A metaphysics which rejects them has failed, in the same way as physical science has failed when it is unable to harmonise them into its theory.

Science only renders the metaphysical need more urgent. In itself it contributes little directly to the solution of the metaphysical problem. But it does contribute something, namely, the exposition of the fact that our experience of sensible apparent things is capable of being analysed into a scientific theory, a theory not indeed complete, but giving every promise of indefinite expansion. This achievement emphasises the intimate relation between our logical thought and the facts of sensible apprehension. Also the special form of scientific theory is bound to have some influence. In the past false science has been the parent of bad metaphysics. After all, science embodies a rigorous scrutiny of one part of the whole evidence from which metaphysicians deduce their conclusions.

CHAPTER X

Space, Time, and Relativity

Fundamental problems concerning space and time have been considered from the standpoints created by many different sciences. The object of this paper is the humble one of bringing some of these standpoints into relation with each other. This necessitates a very cursory treatment of each point of view.

Mathematical physicists have evolved their theory of relativity to explain the negative results of the Morley-Michelson experiment and of the Trouton experiment. Experimental psychologists have considered the evolution of spatial ideas from the crude sense-data of experience. Metaphysicians have considered the majestic uniformity of space and time, without beginning and without end, without boundaries, and without exception in the truths concerning them; all these qualities the more arresting to our attention from the confused accidental nature of the empirical universe which is conditioned by them. Mathematicians have studied the axioms of geometry, and can now deduce all that is believed to be universally true of space and of time by the strictest logic from a limited number of assumptions.

These various lines of thought have been evolved with surprisingly little interconnection. Perhaps it is as well. The results of science are never quite true. By a healthy independence of thought perhaps we sometimes avoid adding other people's errors to our own. But there can be no doubt that the normal method of cross-fertilising thought is by considering the same, or allied problems to our own, in the form which they assume in other sciences.

Here I do not propose to enter into a systematic study of these various chapters of science. I have neither the knowledge nor the time.

First, let us take the ultimate basis of any theory of relativity. All space measurement is from stuff in space to stuff in space. The geometrical entities of empty space never appear. The only geometrical properties of which we have any direct knowledge are properties of those shifting, changeable appearances which we call things in space. It is the sun which is distant, and the ball which is round, and the lamp-posts which are in linear order. Wherever mankind may have got its idea of an infinite unchangeable space from, it is safe to say that it is not an immediate deliverance of direct observation.

There are two antagonistic philosophical ways of recognising this conclusion.

One is to affirm that space and time are conditions for sensible experience, that without projection into space and time sensible experience would not exist. Thus, although it may be true to say that our knowledge of space and time is given in experience, it is not true to say that it is deduced from experience in the same sense that the Law of Gravitation is so deduced. It is not deduced, because in the act of experiencing we are necessarily made aware of space as an infinite given whole, and of time as an unending uniform succession. This philosophical position is expressed by saying that space and time are *a priori* forms of sensibility.

The opposed philosophical method of dealing with the question is to affirm that our concepts of time and space are deductions from experience, in exactly the same way as the Law of Gravitation is such a deduction. If we form exact concepts of points, lines and surfaces, and of successive instants of time, and assume them to be related as expressed by the axioms of geometry and the axioms for time, then we find that we have framed a concept which, with all the exactness of which our observations are capable, expresses the facts of experience.

These two philosophic positions are each designed to explain a certain difficulty. The *a priori* theory explains the absolute universality ascribed to the laws of space and time, a universality not ascribed to any deduction from experience. The experiential theory explains the derivation of the space-time concepts without introducing any other factors beyond those which are admittedly present in framing the other concepts of physical science.

But we have not yet done with the distinctions which in any discussion of space or time must essentially be kept in mind. Put aside the above question as to how these space-time concepts are related to experience—What are they when they are formed?

We may conceive of the points of space as self-subsistent entities which have the indefinable relation of being occupied by the ultimate stuff (matter, I will call it) which is there. Thus, to say that the sun is *there* (wherever it is) is to affirm the relation of occupation between the set of positive and negative electrons which we call the sun and a certain set of points, the points having an existence essentially independent of the sun. This is the absolute theory of space. The absolute theory is not popular just now, but it has very respectable authority on its side—Newton, for one—so treat it tenderly.

The other theory is associated with Leibniz. Our space concepts are concepts of relations between things in space. Thus there is no such entity as a self-subsistent point. A point is merely the name for some peculiarity of the relations between the matter which is, in common language, said to be in space.

It follows from the relative theory that a point should be definable in terms of the relations between material things. So far as I am aware, this outcome of the theory has escaped the notice of mathematicians, who have invariably assumed the point as the ultimate starting ground of their reasoning. Many years ago I explained some types of ways in which we might achieve such a definition, and more recently have added some others. Similar explanations apply to time. Before the theories of space and time have been carried to a satisfactory conclusion on the relational basis, a long and careful scrutiny of the definitions of points of space and instants of time will have to be undertaken, and many ways of effecting these definitions will have to be tried and compared. This is an unwritten chapter of mathematics, in much the same state as was the theory of parallels in the eighteenth century.

In this connection I should like to draw attention to the analogy between time and space. In analysing our experience we distinguish events, and we also distinguish things whose changing relations form the events. If I had time it would be interesting to consider more closely these concepts of events and of things. It must suffice now to point out that things have certain relations to each other which we consider as relations between the space extensions of the things; for example, one space can contain the other, or exclude it, or overlap it. A point in space is nothing else than a certain set of relations between spatial extensions.

Analogously, there are certain relations between events which we express by saying that they are relations between the temporal durations of these events, that is, between the temporal extension of the events. [The durations of two events A and B may one precede the other, or may partially overlap, or may one contain the other, giving in all six possibilities.] The properties of the extension of an event in time are largely analogous to the extension of an object in space. Spatial extensions are expressed by relations between objects, temporal extensions by relations between events.

The point in time is a set of relations between temporal extensions. It needs very little reflection to convince us that a point in time is no direct deliverance of experience. We live in durations, and not in points. But what community, beyond the mere name, is there between extension in time and extension in space? In view of the intimate connection between time and space revealed by the modern theory of relativity, this question has taken on a new importance.

I have not thought out an answer to this question. I suggest, however, that time and space embody those relations between objects on which depends our judgment of their externality to ourselves. Namely, location in space and location in time both embody and perhaps necessitate a judgment of externality. This suggestion is very vague, and I must leave it in this crude form.

Diverse Euclidean Measure Systems

Turning now to the mathematical investigations on the axioms of geometry, the outcome, which is most important for us to remember, is the great separation which it discloses between non-metrical projective geometry, and metrical geometry. Non-metrical projective geometry is by far the more fundamental. Starting with the concepts of points, straight lines, and planes (of which not all three need be taken as indefinable), and with certain very simple non-metrical properties of these entities—such as, for instance, that two points uniquely determine a straight line—nearly the whole of geometry can be constructed. Even quantitative co-ordinates can be introduced, to facilitate the reasoning. But no mention of distance, area, or volume, need have been introduced. Points will have an order on the line, but order does not imply any settled distance.

When we now inquire what measurements of distance are possible, we find that there are different systems of measurement all equally possible. There are three main types of system: any system of one type gives Euclidean geometry, any system of another type gives Hyperbolic (or Lobatchewskian) geometry, any system of the third type gives Elliptic geometry. Also different beings, or the same being if he chooses, may reckon in different systems of the same type, or in systems of different types. Consider the example which will interest us later. Two beings, A and B, agree to use the same three intersecting lines as axes of x, y, z. They both employ a system of measurement of the Euclidean type, and (what is not necessarily the case) agree as to the plane at infinity. That is, they agree as to the lines which are parallel. Then with the usual method of rectangular Cartesian axes, they agree that the coordinates of P are the lengths ON, NM, MP. So far all is harmony. A fixes on the segment OU_1, on Ox, as being the unit length, and B on the segment OV_1, on Ox. A calls his coordinates (x,y,z), and B calls them (X,Y,Z).

Then it is found [since both systems are Euclidean] that, whatever point P be taken,

$$X = \beta x, \ Y = \gamma y, \ Z = \delta z. \ [\beta \neq \gamma \neq \delta.]$$

They proceed to adjust their differences, and first take the x-coordinates. Obviously they have taken different units of length along Ox. The length OU_1, which A calls one unit, B calls β *units*. B changes his unit length to OU_1, from its original length OV_1, and obtains $X = x$. But now, as he must use the same unit for all his measurements, his other coordinates are altered in the same ratio. Thus we now have

$$X = x, \ Y = \gamma y / \beta, \ Z = \delta z / \beta.$$

The fundamental divergence is now evident. A and B agree as to their units along Ox. They settled that by taking along that axis a given segment OU, as having the unit length. But they cannot agree as to what segment along Oy is equal to OU$_1$. A says it is OU$_2$, and B that it is OU$_2'$. Similarly for lengths along OZ.

The result is that A's spheres

$$x^2 + y^2 + z^2 = r^2,$$

are B's ellipsoids,

$$X^2 + \beta^2 Y^2 / \gamma^2 + \beta^2 Z^2 / \delta^2 = r^2,$$

i.e.
$$X^2 / \beta^2 + Y^2 / \gamma^2 + Z^2 / \delta^2 = r^2 / \beta^2.$$

Thus the measurement of angles by the two is hopelessly at variance.

If $\beta \neq \gamma \neq \delta$, there is one, and only one, set of common rectangular axes at O, namely that from which they started. If $\gamma = \delta$, but $\beta \neq \gamma$, then there are a singly infinite number of common rectangular axes found by rotating the axes round Ox. This is, for us, the interesting case. The same phenomena are reproduced by transferring to any parallel axes.

The root of the difficulty is, that A's measuring rod, which for him is a rigid invariable body, appears to B as changing in length when turned in different directions. Similarly all measuring rods, satisfactory to A, violate B's immediate judgment of invariability, and change according to the same law. There is no way out of the difficulty. Two rods ρ and σ coincide whenever laid one on the other; ρ is held still, and both men agree that it does not change. But σ is turned round. A says it is invariable, B says it changes. To test the matter ρ is turned round to measure it, and exactly fits it. But while A is satisfied, B declares that ρ has changed in exactly the same way as did σ. Meanwhile B has procured two material rods satisfactory to him as invariable, and A makes exactly the same objections.

We shall say that A and B employ diverse Euclidean metrical systems.

The most extraordinary fact of human life is that all beings seem to form their judgments of spatial quantity according to the same metrical system. This statement, however, is only true within the limits of accuracy obtained by human observation. When we endeavour to frame a self consistent physical theory we have to admit that diverse spatio-temporal systems of measurement are relevant to the behaviour of things.

Thus estimates of quantity in space and time, and, to some extent, even estimates of order, depend on the individual observer. But what are the crude deliverances of sensible experience, apart from that world of imaginative reconstruction which for each of us has the best claim to be called our real world? Here the experimental psychologist steps in. We cannot get away from him. I wish we could, for he is frightfully difficult to understand. Also, sometimes his knowledge of the principles of mathematics is rather weak, and I sometimes suspect———— No, I will not say what I sometimes think: probably he, with equal reason, is thinking the same sort of thing of us.

I will, however, venture to summarise conclusions, which are, I believe, in harmony with the experimental evidence, both physical and psychological, and which are certainly suggested by the materials for that unwritten chapter in mathematical logic which I have already commended to your notice. The concepts of space and time and of quantity are capable of analysis into bundles of simpler concepts. In any given sensible experience it is not necessary, or even usual, that the whole complete bundle of such concepts apply. For example, the concept of externality may apply without that of linear order, and the concept of linear order may apply without that of linear distance.

Again, the abstract mathematical concept of a space-relation may confuse together distinct concepts which apply to the given perceptions. For example, linear order in the sense of a linear projection from the observer is distinct from linear order in the sense of a row of objects stretching across the line of sight.

Mathematical physics assumes a given world of definitely related objects, and the various space-time systems are alternative ways of expressing those relations as concepts in a form which also applies to the immediate experience of observers.

Yet there must be one way of expressing the relations between objects in a common external world. Alternative methods can only arise as the result of alternative standpoints; that is to say, as the result of leaving something added by the observer sticking (as it were) in the universe.

But this way of conceiving the world of physical science, as composed of hypothetical objects, leaves it as a mere fairy tale. What is really actual are the immediate experiences. The task of deductive science is to consider the concepts which apply to these data of experience, and then to consider the concepts relating to these concepts, and so on to any necessary degree of refinement. As our concepts become more abstract, their logical relations become more general, and less liable to exception. By this logical construction we finally arrive at conceptions, (i) which have determinate exemplifications in the experience of the individuals, and (ii) whose logical relations have a peculiar smoothness. For example, conceptions of mathematical time, of mathematical space, are such smooth conceptions. No one lives in "an infinite given whole," but in a set of fragmentary experiences. The problem is to exhibit the concepts of mathematical space and time as the necessary outcome of these fragments by a process of logical building up. Similarly for the other physical concepts. This process builds a common world of conceptions out of fragmentary worlds of experience. The material pyramids of Egypt are a conception, what is actual are the fragmentary experiences of the races who have gazed on them.

So far as science seeks to rid itself of hypothesis, it cannot go beyond these general logical constructions. For science, as thus conceived, the divergent time orders mentioned above present no difficulty. The different time systems simply register the different relations of the mathematical construct to those individual experiences (actual or hypothetical) which could exist as the crude material from which the construct is elaborated.

But after all it should be possible to elaborate the mathematical construct so as to eliminate specific reference to particular experiences. Whatever be the data of experience, there must be something which can be said of them as a whole, and that something is a statement of the general properties of the common world. It is hard to believe that with proper generalisation time and space will not be found among such properties.

If I understand Kant rightly—which I admit to be very problematical—he holds that in the act of experience we are aware of space and time as ingredients necessary for the occurrence of experience. I would suggest—rather timidly—that this doctrine should be given a different twist, which in fact turns it in the opposite direction—namely, that in the act of experience we perceive a whole formed of related differentiated parts. The relations between these parts possess certain characteristics, and time and space are the expressions of some of the characteristics of these relations. Then the generality and uniformity which are ascribed to time and space express what may be termed the uniformity of the texture of experience.

The success of mankind—modest though it is—in deducing uniform laws of nature is, so far as it goes, a testimony that this uniformity of texture goes beyond those characteristics of the data of experience which are expressed as time and space. Time and space are necessary to experience in the sense that they are characteristics of our experience; and, of course, no one can have our experience without running into them. I cannot see that Kant's deduction amounts to much more than saying that "what is, is"—true enough, but not very helpful.

But I admit that what I have termed the "uniformity of the texture of experience" is a most curious and arresting fact. I am quite ready to believe that it is a mere illusion; and later on in the paper I suggest that this uniformity does not belong to the immediate relations of the crude data of experience, but is the result of substituting for them more refined logical entities, such as relations between relations, or classes of relations, or classes of classes of relations. By this means it can be demonstrated—I think—that the uniformity which must be ascribed to experience is of a much more abstract attenuated character than is usually allowed. This process of lifting the uniform time and space of the physical world into the status of logical abstractions has also the advantage of recognising another fact, namely, the extremely fragmentary nature of all direct individual conscious experience.

My point in this respect is that fragmentary individual experiences are all that we know, and that all speculation must start from these *disjecta membra* as its sole datum. It is not true that we are directly aware of a smooth running world, which in our speculations we are to conceive as given. In my view the creation of the world is the first unconscious act of speculative thought; and the first task of a self-conscious philosophy is to explain how it has been done.

There are roughly two rival explanations. One is to assert the world as a postulate. The other way is to obtain it as a deduction, not a deduction through a chain of reasoning, but a deduction through a chain of definitions which, in fact, lifts thought on to a more abstract level in which the logical ideas are more complex, and their relations are more universal. In this way the broken limited experiences sustain that connected infinite world in which in our thoughts we live. There are more remarks while on this point I wish to make—

(i) The fact that immediate experience is capable of this deductive superstructure must mean that it itself has a certain uniformity of texture. So this great fact still remains.

(ii) I do not wish to deny the world as a postulate. Speaking without prejudice, I do not see how in our present elementary state of philosophical advance we can get on without middle axioms, which, in fact, we habitually assume.

My position is, that by careful scrutiny we should extrude such postulates from every part of our organised knowledge in which it is possible to do without them.

Now, physical science organises our knowledge of the relations between the deliverances of our various senses. I hold that in this department of knowledge such postulates, though not entirely to be extruded, can be reduced to a minimum in the way which I have described.

We note again that the relational theory of space from another point of view brings us back to the idea of the fundamental space-entities as being logical constructs from the relations between things. The difference is, that this paragraph is written from a more developed point of view, as it implicitly assumes the things in space, and conceives space as an expression of certain of their relations. Combining this paragraph with what has gone before, we see that the suggested procedure is first to define "things" in terms of the data of experience, and then to define space in terms of the relations between things.

I emphasise the point that our only exact data as to the physical world are our sensible perceptions. We must not slip into the fallacy of assuming that we are comparing a given world with given perceptions of it. The physical world is, in some general sense of the term, a deduced concept.

Our problem is, in fact, to fit the world to our perceptions, and not our perceptions to the world.